MATT AND TOM OLDFIELD

Cumbria

County Council

Libraries, books and more..........

Please return/renew this item by the last date shown.
Library items may also be renewed by phone on
030 33 33 1234 (24hours) or via our website

www.cumbria.gov.uk/libraries

Cumbria Libraries

CLIC

Interactive Catalogue

Ask for a CLIC password

Published by Dino Books
an imprint of John Blake Publishing
3 Bramber Court, 2 Bramber Road,
London W14 9PB, England

www.johnblakepublishing.co.uk

www.facebook.com/johnblakebooks 🇫
twitter.com/jblakebooks 🇪

This edition published in 2018

ISBN: 978 1 78606 923 8

British Library Cataloguing-in-Publication Data:

A catalogue record for this book is available from the British Library.

Design by www.envydesign.co.uk

Printed in Great Britain by Clays Ltd, St Ives plc

1 3 5 7 9 10 8 6 4 2

Papers used by John Blake Publishing are natural, recyclable products made from
wood grown in sustainable forests. The manufacturing processes conform to the
environmental regulations of the country of origin.

Every attempt has been made to contact the relevant copyright-holders, but some
were unobtainable. We would be grateful if the appropriate people could contact us.

John Blake Publishing is an imprint of Bonnier Publishing.
www.bonnierpublishing.co.uk

For Noah and Nico,
Southampton's future strikeforce

Matt Oldfield is an accomplished writer and the editor-in-chief of football review site *Of Pitch & Page*. Tom Oldfield is a freelance sports writer and the author of biographies on Cristiano Ronaldo, Arsène Wenger and Rafael Nadal.

Cover illustration by Dan Leydon.
To learn more about Dan visit danleydon.com
To purchase his artwork visit etsy.com/shop/footynews
Or just follow him on Twitter @danleydon

TABLE OF CONTENTS

ACKNOWLEDGEMENTS

First of all, I'd like to thank John Blake Publishing –
and particularly my editor James Hodgkinson – for
giving me the opportunity to work on these books
and for supporting me throughout. Writing stories for
the next generation of football fans is both an honour
and a pleasure.

I wouldn't be doing this if it wasn't for Tom. I
owe him so much and I'm very grateful for his belief
in me as an author. I feel like Robin setting out on a
solo career after a great partnership with Batman. I
hope I do him (Tom, not Batman) justice with these
new books.

Next up, I want to thank my friends for keeping

me sane during long hours in front of the laptop. Pang, Will, Mills, Doug, John, Charlie – the laughs and the cups of coffee are always appreciated.

I've already thanked my brother but I'm also very grateful to the rest of my family, especially Melissa, Noah and of course Mum and Dad. To my parents, I owe my biggest passions: football and books. They're a real inspiration for everything I do.

Finally, I couldn't have done this without Iona's encouragement and understanding during long, work-filled weekends. Much love to you.

CHAPTER 1

PRIDE OF PORTUGAL

World Cup 2006, Germany, 5 July 2006

Growing up in Portugal's 'Golden Generation' with Rui Costa and João Pinto, Luís had always dreamed of World Cup glory. They won the Under-17 Euros and then the Under-20 World Cup, but could they go on and win the real thing? The nation had great expectations – Portugal had never won the World Cup, not even in the golden days of 'The King', Eusébio.

Was this Portugal's best chance? Forty years after Eusébio, Portugal had another chance – they were back in the semi-finals again with Luís and his teammates. They were one huge match away from the World Cup Final. Of his 'Golden Generation', Luís was the last man standing. He was now his country's experienced captain and his job was to guide Portugal's new generation to victory. This was his last tournament, his last try, and he wanted to go out with a bang.

At club level, with Barcelona, Real Madrid and Inter Milan, he had won everything – the Spanish League, the Italian League *and* the Champions League. He had even won the Ballon d'Or, football's greatest individual prize. But for his country? A Euro 2004 runners-up medal was all he had to show for fifteen years of dedication. Luís couldn't bear to end his international career empty-handed.

'Come on!' he shouted in the tunnel, looking back at his teammates, Pauleta, Deco, Maniche and Cristiano Ronaldo.

With top talent like those players, Luís knew that Portugal were good enough to win. It wouldn't be easy, however, especially against a team like France.

'Are you ready for this?' a voice asked him.

It was his old Real Madrid teammate, Zinedine

Zidane. Luís was the captain of Portugal and Zinedine was the captain of France. Two of the world's greatest footballers were about to do battle for the last time. In the Euro 2000 semi-final, Zinedine had come out on top, but Luís would do everything possible to stop that from happening again.

'You bet, Zizou!' he replied, leaning over to hug his friend.

After the national anthems, the players moved into their positions for kick-off. There was nothing left to say. Luís had already delivered his message in the dressing room: 'Let's show the world that we've learnt our lessons from Euro 2000 and 2004. I want cool, calm heads all over the pitch. Yes?'

'Yes!' his teammates boomed back.

'We belong at this level!'

Portugal started well. France's goalkeeper Fabien Barthez had to make good saves to stop Deco and Maniche.

'That's it!' Luís clapped encouragingly. 'Keep this up, guys!'

When he got the ball from Miguel, it was Luís's

turn to attack. He dribbled forward at speed, always looking around for a clever pass. As Patrick Vieira rushed over to tackle him, Luís decided to shoot. The Portugal fans shuffled in their seats, ready to celebrate. It was a decent effort but not good enough to beat Barthez.

'Ohhhhhhhhhhhhhhhhhhhhhhhhh!' the fans groaned in disappointment.

At the other end, Florent Malouda passed to Thierry Henry. As Henry turned on the edge of the box, Ricardo Carvalho slipped and tripped him. Penalty!

'Not again!' Luís thought to himself.

France had also won the match at Euro 2000 with a penalty. Six years later, Zinedine was about to step up to the spot once more. Like Luís, Zinedine never felt the pressure. 1–0 to France!

'Don't panic!' Luís urged his teammates. 'We've got plenty of time.'

That time, however, raced by and there was no equaliser for Portugal. Luís passed to Pauleta, who shot just wide. Cristiano's free kick swerved through the air and Barthez spilled it. Luís was there in the penalty area and the ball was coming straight towards him. He leapt up high, but he couldn't keep his header down. It landed on the roof of the net.

'Noooo!' Luís cried out with his arms covering his head.

'Noooo!' Cristiano screamed up at the sky.

Luís didn't give up. He kept trying to create chances until the referee blew that dreaded final whistle. Portugal 0 France 1.

It was over. Luís's World Cup adventures were over. He had done his best to lead Portugal to glory but, in the end, his best just wasn't enough. Luís felt crushed. In that awful moment, it was easy to forget just how far Portugal had come since his international debut in 1991 – from nowhere, all the way to the World Cup semi-final.

Luís walked around the pitch, thanking the fans for all their support. They knew that he had given everything for his country. Luís was a national hero, the Pride of Portugal. That's why they chanted his name.

Figo! Figo! Figo!

'It's your turn now,' he told his protégé, Cristiano. 'It's your turn to be Portugal's leader. Do what I couldn't quite do – win the World Cup!'

That had been Luís's dream ever since his early days in Almada.

CHAPTER 2

AN ONLY CHILD IN ALMADA

António caught the ball and rolled it back to his son. 'Right Luís, one more shot and then I really need to get going,' he said.

It was a Saturday morning and he had errands to run in Lisbon. The Figos lived in Almada, just across the Tagus River from Portugal's famous capital. The striking 25 de Abril Bridge connected the two cities. António and his wife, Maria Joana, had grown up in the south of the country but before their son was born, they moved further north; there were better job opportunities around Lisbon.

The smile on Luís's face fell into a frown. How was he supposed to play football on his own? He kicked the ball moodily towards his dad.

António felt awful. At times like this, it was hard for an only child like Luís. He needed friends to play with.

'I'm sorry, son. I'd love to stay out here with you, but what would your mum say? I'll tell you what she'd say. She'd say, "António, why haven't you fixed the kitchen sink? You said you'd do it weeks ago!"'

He hoped that his silly impression of his wife would make Luís laugh, and it worked.

'Hey, why don't you come to the shops with me?' António asked hopefully. 'Who knows, maybe we'll get an ice cream…?'

Luís shook his head. He would rather just kick his football around instead. That was his favourite thing to do. If he didn't have someone to play with, he would just have to pretend. He was used to dribbling past imaginary defenders and shooting past imaginary goalkeepers.

António shrugged and was about to go inside. But further down the street, he could hear the shouts and cheers of a football match going on. He stopped and turned around. 'Shall we go and take a quick look?' he asked.

This time, Luís nodded. He was only six years old, but he was brave and ready to test his skills against the big boys.

The big boys didn't turn out to be that big, after all. They were making lots of noise, but most of them weren't much older than Luís. They weren't much better than him at football either.

As they stood on the side watching, António recognised one of the boys. He lived on the same street as the Figos. It was a friendly neighbourhood, where people knew and helped each other.

'Hi Dani!' António called out.

The boy turned and waved politely. 'Hi, Mr Figo!'

António pushed his son forward. 'Do you think Luís here could join in your game please? I know he's still young but he's a talented little player!'

Luís looked down at his own feet and waited for Dani's answer. On the one hand, he felt very shy around these new kids, but on the other hand, he was desperate to play. He crossed his fingers behind his back.

Dani looked over at the other boys and did a head count. It was five against six. 'Right guys, this is Luís and he'll be on my team!' he called out. Then he shook hands with Luís and pointed out their teammates.

António thanked Dani and whispered, 'Please look after him!'

Then he went over and gave his son a hug. 'Do you think you'll be happy here for a bit?'

Luís nodded eagerly.

'Great, I'll be back in an hour. If you need anything, your mum is at home. Good luck!'

In the end, his dad was gone for more than an hour, but Luís didn't notice. He was too busy having the time of his life. For the first ten minutes, he did a lot of running around without touching the ball. The others ignored him as if he was invisible.

'Over here!' he cried. 'Over here!'

Luís didn't give up, though. After a few good tackles, his teammates started to trust him. Dani passed the ball to Luís and he passed to William, who scored. They were working well together.

'Great work!' Dani cheered, giving Luís a high-five.

That filled Luís with confidence. The next time he got the ball, he dribbled forward and sped past the first defender. He could see the next defender coming towards him, the biggest boy in the match. Luís looked up and hit a perfect cross into Dani's path.

'Wow, you've got skills!' the goalscorer said, looking impressed.

Luís smiled and got ready to go again. He could happily play football all day.

After a few nice assists, he focused on getting a goal of his own. But that wouldn't be easy, now that his opponents knew how good he was. They certainly weren't taking it easy on the little guy any more.

'Come on, you didn't even try to get the ball there!' Dani protested.

Luís's knee was bleeding from the fall, but he picked himself up and played on. He couldn't stop yet, not until he'd scored at least one goal.

Luís passed inside to Dani. 'One-two!' he shouted

and kept on running towards goal.

When the return pass arrived, he was through, with just the goalkeeper to beat. When should he shoot? Now? No – Luís calmly dribbled round the keeper and tapped it in between the jumpers.

*Goooooooooooooooaaaaaaaaaaaaalllllllllllllllllllllllllllllllllll
llll!!!!!!!!!!!!!!!!!!!!!!!*

He felt on top of the world, but he kept his excitement to himself. No-one else really celebrated their goals, and he was hoping to get invited back to play again.

'Yes, Luís!' someone cheered from the pavement.

Who was it? It was his dad! António had arrived just in time to see Luís's wondergoal. It was a proud moment for father and son.

'Thanks, Dani!' António said as they left to go home for lunch.

'Yeah, thanks, Dani!' Luís added.

'No problem, it was great to have you. Come back next weekend – same time, same place. We need awesome players like you!'

CHAPTER 3

STREET SKILLS

After that great start, Luís just got better and better. He was a very good passer and a cool finisher, but it was his dribbling skills that really made him stand out from the rest. When he was on the run, none of his new friends could tackle him, not even if they all worked together. Luís twisted and turned, using his right foot then his left then his right again, but he never lost the ball.

'How do you do it?' Dani asked, his voice full of frustration. He had just spent a whole match trying and failing to keep Luís quiet. 'You look like you're moving at half-speed and there's never any space on this pitch. I should be able to stop you, but I can't! So, come on, what's your secret?'

Luís smiled and shrugged. How was he supposed to explain his natural talent? He played football for hours every day, but that was just for fun, and to test the silky skills that he was born with.

In the streets and sandy playgrounds of Almada, Luís tormented defender after defender. Some of them walked away in shock, feeling dizzy. Some of them stormed off, annoyed and embarrassed. And some of them gave up on tackling Luís and started kicking him instead.

'Hey, you can't just hack his ankles!'

His teammates tried to protect him, but Luís didn't really need looking after. He stayed calm and determined, no matter what.

Luís knew that when his opponents started fouling him, he had won the battle. They couldn't handle him fairly, so they resorted to cheating instead. But if his fancy footwork was good enough, even the heavy lunges couldn't stop Luís. That was his challenge.

Challenge accepted! Luís hurdled over slide-tackles, dodged shoulder barges and wriggled away from shirt pulls. It was all good practice for the next step in his football career – playing for a proper team in competitive matches.

Luís was desperate to get going.

'If I'm going to be a professional when I'm older,' he told his dad with a serious look on his young face, 'I need to test myself at a higher level.'

António nodded, trying not to laugh. His son was only ten years old and he was already talking like an adult.

He clapped his hands together. 'Right son, well let's find you a team then!'

It didn't take long for them to find one, and they didn't have to travel far. In fact, the team came to Luís.

José Silva was the President of União Futebol Clube, or 'Os Pastilhas' as the people of Almada called it. The club's coaches often went out to watch kids playing in the local area, as it was a great way to discover new talent.

One day, Silva stopped to watch a boy running rings around his friends in the street. The scene wasn't unusual, but the talent was. The boy had an excellent, delicate first touch and he dribbled so gracefully with the ball, gliding past his opponents. It was a joy to watch.

When the game finished, Silva went over to speak to the star. 'Hello – well played out there. You've got street skills! My name is José and I'm the President of Os Pastilhas. What's your name?'

'Luís Figo,' the boy replied, looking very serious.

'Nice to meet you, Luís! How would you feel about coming to play for Os Pastilhas? We could use someone like you in our futsal team.'

'Yes, I'd like that,' Luís said, trying to contain his excitement.

'Great, well, if you let me know your address, I'd like to speak to your parents and make sure that they're happy with it.'

António was more than happy with it; he was delighted. 'My son is going to play for Sporting one day!' he proudly predicted.

Maria Joana, however, was worried. 'What about his schoolwork?' she asked her husband. 'He already spends his whole time thinking about football, and this will only make things worse. Studying is important. I want him to get a good education!'

After a long discussion, Luís's parents decided to let him play for Os Pastilhas. There were strict conditions, however.

'You can only go to training once you've finished your homework. Okay?'

'Yes, Mum.'

'And if any of your school grades slip, you won't be able to play anymore. Okay?'

'Yes, Dad.'

With that agreement in place, Luís was ready to kick off his Os Pastilhas career. He couldn't wait.

It didn't take long for him to shine. His street skills came in very handy, especially playing with a smaller, heavier ball. To be a good futsal player, you needed to have great close control and technique in tight spaces. Luís had both by the bucketload.

'Brilliant work!' José Silva cheered from the sidelines.

The Os Pastilhas president was very pleased with his new signing. It was early days, but Luís already looked like a superstar in the making.

CHAPTER 4

WORLD CUP HEROES

The 1982 World Cup was the tournament that changed Luís's life. He was nine years old at the time, the perfect age to first experience the wonders of twenty-four countries competing against each other to win international football's greatest prize.

'I love it!' Luís told his dad as they watched the matches at home on TV.

It helped that the World Cup was taking place nearby in Spain. Some of the matches were even played in Vigo, just an hour's drive from the Portuguese border. That made everything much more exciting.

The football was very exciting too. There were so

many amazing players on show. Luís liked France's midfielder Michel Platini and Italy's striker Paolo Rossi, but his favourites were the Number 10s Diego Maradona, from Argentina, and Zico, from Brazil. He loved their South American style.

Maradona had so many tricks up his sleeve. When he dribbled with the ball, the defenders just could not get it off him. It was like the ball was stuck to his foot.

'How does he do that?' Luís marvelled. 'He's magic!'

'Just keep practising and you'll get there,' his dad encouraged him.

The Argentine's second goal against Hungary was certainly magic. After a great one-two, Maradona burst into the box and slammed a fierce left-foot shot into the bottom corner.

'What a goal!' Luís shouted, jumping up and down on the sofa.

Zico's goals were even better. The Brazilian scored an unbelievable free kick against Scotland and then an acrobatic volley against New Zealand.

Even his dad was impressed. 'Wow, this team

could give Pelé's Brazil a run for their money!'

The Figos watched as many games as they possibly could together. Sadly, neither Maradona's Argentina nor Zico's Brazil made it to the semi-finals, but Italy were worthy winners in the end.

The only bad thing about the 1982 World Cup was that Portugal weren't in it. For the fourth tournament in a row, they hadn't qualified.

'Why are we so bad?' Luís asked his dad.

'I don't know but we used to be good, I promise!' António replied. 'Have you heard of Eusébio?'

Luís rolled his eyes. There wasn't a single person in Portugal who didn't know about Eusébio. His dad talked about 'The King' all the time.

'Well, when we had Eusébio, we were brilliant. I wish you could have seen that 1966 World Cup! I can still remember it like it was yesterday. We reached the semi-finals and we should have won it. Eusébio scored nine goals in that tournament. Nine – that's a whole hat-trick more than Rossi!'

It wasn't all doom and gloom for Portugal, however. After the disappointment of missing the

1982 World Cup, they bounced back quickly and qualified for Euro 84.

With the Figos cheering them on, Portugal got all the way to the semi-finals. There, they lost to the hosts, France, and even then only because of a Platini goal in the last minute of extra time.

It was a cruel blow but suddenly, Luís and his friends had new heroes and this time, they were from their own country.

Some of the boys wanted to be the Portugal captain and goalkeeper Manuel Bento and others wanted to be Rui Jordão, their goalscoring hero. Luís, however, preferred Fernando Chalana. Chalana was a quick and skilful winger who could play on either side and kick with either foot.

'He's awesome,' Luís argued to his friends. 'I'm going to be just like him when I'm older!'

Chalana had set up both of Jordão's goals against France. For the first, he chipped a perfect left-wing cross into the box, and right on to his striker's head. By the time Portugal scored their second, Chalana had switched to the other side. He faked to kick it with his left foot and then moved it cleverly on to his right instead.

Olé!

The French left-back was totally fooled. Chalana's cross looped all the way to the back post, where Jordão volleyed it in.

After all that Euro 84 excitement, Portugal then qualified for the 1986 World Cup, their first appearance since Eusébio's starring role in 1966. Luís was so excited as the tournament started.

'I think we've got a good chance,' he told his dad. 'We should get to the quarter-finals, at least.'

Chalana was no longer in the squad, but Luís had a new hero on the left wing to admire – Paulo Futre. Futre was even better at dribbling and his nickname was 'The Portuguese Maradona'.

'Do you know where Futre started his career?' António asked his son before Portugal's first match against England.

Luís shrugged.

'Sporting!' his dad answered proudly. The Figos were big fans of 'The Lions', Sporting Lisbon.

Portugal beat England, but then lost to Poland and Morocco. They finished bottom of the group. After only three matches, their 1986 World Cup was over.

'I can't believe it!' Luís cried out. 'I really thought we would do well.'

António put an arm around his son's shoulder. 'I've learnt that it's best to fear the worst as a Portugal fan. When expectations are high, we're hopeless!'

As Luís turned off the TV, he felt disappointed but also inspired. This time, Portugal had failed to win the World Cup, but they would have other shots at glory. What the country needed was a full team of football talent, rather than just a few star players. What they needed was a Golden Generation, and Luís was determined to be a part of it.

CHAPTER 5

YOUNG LION

In the end, Luís only stayed at Os Pastilhas for one season. It wasn't that he didn't enjoy playing futsal for his local team; it was just that he got a better offer elsewhere.

'Welcome, everyone!' Aurélio Pereira announced, trying to sound as friendly as possible.
Sadly, Pereira's smile didn't reassure the boys' nerves.

Pereira was the head of Sporting Lisbon's new youth system. He had two main jobs – discovering new talent, and then turning that talent into top professional players.

'Here at Sporting, our aim isn't just to win championships,' he told the boys. 'We also want to train players that can go on to play for the national team!'

Luís really liked the sound of that. He wasn't quite as Sporting-mad as his dad, but he was very proud to be Portuguese. That was his ultimate dream – to play for his country, just like Fernando Chalana and Paulo Futre.

'This is where my journey starts,' Luís muttered to himself.

The competition for places didn't bother Luís. Whether there were five thousand other kids or just fifty, he would still have to stand out from the crowd. He knew he could do that. He had been doing that for years. If he got the chance to show what he could do with the ball, Sporting would pick him.

Once the boys had been split up into smaller groups, Pereira walked around, looking for the signs of a superstar. He could never predict what they might be. It was just a feeling, an instinct. Pereira watched Luís during a dribbling drill. Most of the twelve-year-olds knocked a cone or two on their way through, but not Luís. He weaved from side to side, and from foot to foot, with such ease and grace. The ball moved with him, as if it was just an extra part of his foot.

'Did you see that?' Pereira asked one of the youth coaches, João Barnabé. 'That kid's got something special!'

The more Pereira watched Luís, the more impressed he became. It wasn't just his dribbling, or his passing, or his shooting. It was also his character. Under the Sporting pressure, so many of the youngsters froze. They let their nerves get the better of them and let themselves down. But not this kid. Pressure, what pressure? He looked relaxed. It was as if the trial was no different from playing in the street with his mates.

And yet, he also looked so focused and determined. This boy meant business.

'Look at that!' Pereira said to Barnabé, pointing.

'What am I looking at?' the coach asked, sounding confused. Luís was just crouched down, retying the laces on his football boots.

'Look at the way he's tying them,' Pereira

continued. 'How many times have we seen kids do it in a flash, rush back out onto the pitch and then have to do it again a few minutes later? But he's calmly taking his time over the job. He wants to get it just right.'

In a simple task, he had found the signs of a superstar. This boy was different. He was special. Who knew – perhaps he would be the future of Portuguese football.

As the trial ended, the boys drifted back to their waiting parents. Some of them looked pleased and some of them looked disappointed. Either way, they would have to wait for a phone call to see if they had been chosen as one of Sporting's lucky few.

Luís, however, didn't want to wait. He had tried his best, but was it good enough? There was only one way to find out. Before he went home, he walked straight up to Barnabé and asked him the burning question.

'So, am I in?'

The coach was too surprised to speak. Luckily, Pereira was there by his side.

'You're a strong character, aren't you!' he said with a laugh. 'What's your name?'

'Luís Figo.'

'Okay Luís, come back next week to train with our Under-13s. How does that sound?'

'Great, thanks!'

A few weeks later, Luís's Os Pastilhas career was officially over. Luís was a Young Lion now, and his dad was prouder than ever.

CHAPTER 6

THE START OF SOMETHING SPECIAL

Luís glided through the Sporting youth teams like he glided through defences – with speed, skill, style, and lots of cheering fans. Under-13s, Under-14s, Under-15s, Under-16s – there was just no stopping him. Every time he reached the next level, he upped his game. There was nothing that he liked more than a new challenge.

In May 1989, Luís got his first international call-up. He was in Portugal's squad for the Under-16 European Championships.

'I'm going to Denmark,' he told his parents, happily. 'I'll see you when I'm back with the trophy!'

Expectations were growing for Portugal's 'Golden Generation'. Just two months earlier, the Under-20s had won the World Cup in Saudi Arabia. And the year before, their Under-16s had reached the European Championship final, only losing to Spain on penalties. Could they go one better this time?

Luís would do his best to make that happen. He couldn't wait to wear the red-and-green national shirt with pride.

Portugal got off to a great start, easily winning each game in their group. They won 2–0 against Switzerland, then 3–0 against Norway, and then 4–0 against Romania. Luís was their playmaker in midfield. He scored one goal against Norway but mostly he created goals for others in the Portugal squad. Their striker, Gil, was having a field day.

'Thanks!' Gil said, high-fiving Luís after another clever assist. 'You make my job so easy!'

In the semi-final against Spain, Portugal's Under 16s got their revenge after their disappointing final the previous year, and beat them 2–1. Luís delivered the crosses and Gil scored the goals.

'We're in the final!' the whole team cheered together.

Even East Germany couldn't handle Portugal's dangerous duo. Luís dribbled down the left wing and pulled the ball back for Gil. 1–0! Luís added a penalty as they eventually won 4–1.

Campiones, Campiones, Olé, Olé, Olé!

Portugal's Under-16s were the Champions of Europe for the first time ever. The Golden Generation was living up to its name. At the final whistle, the players hugged each other and cried tears of joy. In the space of just two successful weeks, many of them had become best friends.

'This is the start of something special!' the Portugal team cheered as they lifted their manager up into the air.

The FIFA U-16 World Championships were held in Scotland a month later. Luís was really excited to play against the likes of Argentina and Brazil. He still had happy memories of watching them on TV at the 1982 World Cup. Now, seven years later, he was playing against them for real, as a Portuguese youth international. He pinched himself to check that it wasn't all a dream.

In the first round, Luís continued his amazing attacking partnership with Gil. However, as their opponents got tougher, Gil stopped scoring. It was Luís who stepped up, with the team's opening goal against Argentina.

'Come on, we can do this!' he shouted, pumping his fists.

But in the semi-finals against Scotland, Portugal totally ran out of steam. Luís tried again and again to create a moment of magic for his country but it just wasn't their day. As the minutes went by, the home crowd got louder and louder. The Portugal Under-16s trudged off the pitch in Edinburgh, devastated and defeated.

'Keep your head up, kid,' the manager Carlos Queiroz said, putting an arm around Luís's shoulder. 'You should be really proud of that performance.'

Queiroz knew exactly who his star player was. What he needed now were a few more stars, the last pieces in the Portugal puzzle. Ahead of the 1990

Under-18 European Championships, he found them. In came Jorge Costa, a defender from Porto. Back came João Pinto, an attacker from Boavista who had won the World Cup with the Under-20s. And best of all, in came Rui Costa, a midfielder from Benfica.

Luís was impressed by the talent and balance of the team. They now had quality players all over the pitch, and he could tell that everyone wanted to win just as much as he did.

'Right, let's do this!' Queiroz told them confidently.

The stage was set for the Golden Generation to truly shine. However, Portugal's quarter-final against the hosts Hungary went all the way to penalties. Luís had to keep a cool head to score the winning spot-kick.

'We're through,' their manager said, 'but we can play so much better than that. It's Spain next, and they'd love to beat us again!'

Portugal came out firing. All their talent clicked together beautifully. João scored the first and Luís scored the second. That was enough to take them through to the final against the Soviet Union. Portugal were the favourites to win the tournament.

As they prepared for the big game, Luís thought back to the Under-16 final against East Germany. That day, they had been calm and always in control. Portugal needed to find that sweet spot again.

'Come on!' Luís shouted, pumping his fists.

They started the game well, but where was a goal when they needed it? It felt like that Scotland semi-final all over again.

'There's no need to panic yet,' Luís urged his teammates when they started taking wild long-range shots. 'We can still win this playing our normal game!'

In the end, however, Portugal couldn't. The match finished 0–0 and it was time for penalties. Luís took a deep breath, stretched his tired legs and got ready to step up. He was Portugal's best spot-kick taker and his country needed him.

He wasn't the first, however. That was Rui Bento, and he missed! Now there was even more pressure on Luís to score. Luckily, he was the coolest player around. He scored and so did defender Abel Xavier.

Could they still win the shoot-out?

No, because the Soviet Union didn't miss a single penalty. While their players celebrated a shock victory, Luís put his hands on his head and stared down at the grass below his feet. It was a horrible feeling to lose any match, but it was so much worse when it was a final. They had failed.

'How did we throw that away?' Luís moaned.

There was some light at the end of the tunnel, however. By reaching the final, Portugal had qualified for the 1991 FIFA World Youth Championship. They would get the chance to bounce back.

'Guys, we *have* to win it!' Luís told his teammates.

CHAPTER 7

OFF THE MARK AT SPORTING

Meanwhile, back in club football, Luís was getting closer and closer to his Sporting debut. By the age of seventeen, he was practising regularly with the first-team squad. The senior players could see that Luís had the talent to be Portugal's 'next big thing', but did he have the strength to battle with the big boys? That's what Pedro Venâncio wanted to test on the training ground.

Pedro was Sporting's long-serving centre-back, a player with lots of experience and cunning. What he lacked in pace and skill, he made up for in the tackle. The Portuguese League would be full of tough defenders like Pedro. It was the perfect way for Luís to prove that he was ready to be a top professional footballer.

'Bring it on!' he muttered under his breath.

Luís didn't rush into his daring dribbles. Instead, he passed and moved, passed and moved. Everywhere he went, Pedro followed right behind him. It was like a game of chess between the two of them. He hoped that the defender would tire himself out soon.

Luís dropped deeper to get the ball in midfield, and then burst forward at speed. With a stepover and a drop of the shoulder, he zoomed past the defensive midfielder, Oceano da Cruz. He was through on goal, with just Pedro and the keeper to beat.

It was like those street games in Almada all over again. Luís needed to use his skill to get past the centre-back *and* avoid his attempts to foul him. It was a good thing that he had two excellent feet.

As Luís entered the penalty area, he pulled his left leg back to shoot. It was the moment that Pedro had been waiting for. He slid across the grass for a big crunching tackle.

'This will bring that cocky kid back down to earth!' he thought to himself.

But Luís was one step ahead of him. As the defender flew towards him, he calmly switched the ball across to his right foot, and just out of reach. Pedro's boot kicked thin air! Luís had won the battle but he didn't rush the final shot. He looked up and coolly curled the ball into the top corner.

Goooooooooooooooooooooaaaaaaaaaaaaaaalllllllllll llllllllllllllll!!!!!!!!!!!!!!!!!

Pedro picked himself up and looked angrily over at the Sporting manager, Raul Águas. 'He's ready,' was all he said.

In the last few weeks of the 1989–90 season, Sporting sat third in the Portuguese League, a long way behind the top two – Porto and Benfica. The Lions would definitely qualify for the UEFA Cup, so why not give the youngsters a chance?

That's exactly what Águas did. Against Marítimo, he started Paulo Torres at left-back and named Luís and Marinho as substitutes. They were all still teenagers, but Luís was the youngest of them all. He was only seventeen.

'How are you feeling about making your debut?' Pedro asked in the dressing room before the match.

After their training ground battle, they were now good friends.

Luís shrugged. 'I might not even come on,' he replied.

'You will come on, so be ready!' Pedro told him. 'You might only get a few minutes at the end, but every second counts, okay? Show the fans what you can do, and they'll be singing your name in no time.'

Luís nodded and thanked his teammate for the advice.

For eighty minutes, Luís sat fidgeting on the bench, watching and waiting. Would Águas give him his big chance? It looked unlikely while Sporting were only winning 1–0.

Luís slumped in his seat. Why had he got his hopes up? He wasn't the only one who would be disappointed. Aurélio Pereira and João Barnabé, the academy coaches who had helped him to develop his talent, were there in the José Alvalade Stadium.

His parents were there too, expecting to see his first steps as a Lion.

Suddenly, Luís heard his name being called by the assistant manager. 'Figo – warm up!'

He jumped up eagerly and jogged along the touchline, stretching out his legs. He looked up at the area where his parents were, but he couldn't pick out their faces in the crowd.

With five minutes to go in the game, Luís came on for his Sporting debut. He didn't feel nervous as he ran on, he was just excited to be achieving his childhood dream. This was what he had been working so hard for – to wear the famous green-and-white striped shirt.

With his long, curly hair flapping, Luís chased after every ball. He could hear Pedro's words in his head – 'every second counts'. Unfortunately, the five minutes went way too fast, too fast to try even one mazy dribble.

'Next time, kid,' Águas said at the final whistle, patting Luís on the back.

'Next time,' Luís repeated to himself with relief.

That meant he would get another chance to play.

However, that 'next time' didn't come quickly. The new Sporting manager wasn't so interested in the young players. He wanted experienced professionals who could challenge for the Portuguese League title. Luís only played five minutes for the senior team in the whole of the 1990–91 season. It was frustrating to be so close and yet so far from the first team.

'Be patient,' Pedro kept telling him. 'Your time is coming soon!'

In the summer of 1991, it was all change at Sporting. Oceano left and so did right-back Carlos Xavier and star striker Fernando Gomes. It was time for a new young Lion to rise up and shine.

Luís started in the first game of the 1991–92 season and never looked back. The fans loved their galloping young winger. Sporting's new Number 7 was a joy to watch with the ball at his feet.

Figo! Figo! Figo!

Luís had skill, speed, vision and spirit – the only thing missing was goals. He created lots for his teammates, but he couldn't seem to score himself.

'Don't worry, that's not your job,' his manager reassured him. 'Your job is setting up goals and you're doing that brilliantly!'

Still, Luís was desperate to grab his first goal. He had been dreaming about it since he was a young boy. He stood next to the Torreense goalkeeper in the six-yard box, waiting for the corner-kick. He wasn't the best at heading, but he was quite tall and strong.

As the cross came in, Luís jumped high, even higher than the keeper. He flicked the ball on and into the net.

Goooooooooooooooaaaaaaaaaaaaalllllllllllllllllllllllllllllllllll!!!!!!!!!!!!!!!!!!!!!!!!!!!!!

Luís had been waiting a long time for this moment. His first goal, and a header too! It was an unbelievable feeling. He pointed up at the fans and pumped his fists with passion.

'You did it!' his teammate Krasimir Balakov cheered.

'Yes!' Luís roared up at the sky above him.

It felt like a heavy weight had been lifted off Luís's shoulders. Now, he was really off the mark at Sporting.

CHAPTER 8

WORLD CUP GLORY

Luís and his Portugal teammates counted down
the days until the 1991 FIFA World Youth
Championship. They had three big reasons to be
excited.

The first reason was that they were the reigning
champions. In 1989, while Luís had been winning
the Euros with the Under-16s, the Portugal Under-
20s had lifted the World Cup trophy in Saudi Arabia.

The second reason was that two years later, they
still had the best team in the tournament. Luís was
lining up alongside João Pinto, Jorge Costa, Rui Costa
and Rui Bento again, plus his Sporting teammates
Paulo Torres and Emílio Peixe. There were so many

amazing attacking players that Luís had to wear the Number 3 shirt.

'No-one can compete with us!' shouted João, their captain.

The third reason was that Portugal were playing on home soil in front of huge local crowds. It was a massive moment for the country and lifting the trophy would be the icing on the delicious, home-made cake.

With three wins out of three, Portugal cruised through to the quarter-finals. The match against Mexico started spectacularly. Playing in central midfield, Luís threaded a brilliant pass to João, who was fouled in the area. Penalty! Paulo stepped up and scored. 1–0!

Portugal flags were waved all around the Estádio da Luz in Lisbon. Thanks to their Golden Generation, the nation finally had something to cheer about.

But before half-time, Mexico gained a surprise equaliser. Luís and his teammates stood scattered around the penalty area, frozen in shock.

'Who was marking him?' the goalkeeper screamed.

It didn't matter; Portugal just had to recover quickly. In extra time, Toni scored the winning goal and the stadium went wild. They were through!

Not everyone was quite so delighted, however.

'We got lucky tonight,' Queiroz told his players firmly in the dressing room. 'If we play like that again in the semis, our tournament is over!'

The semi-final was tight and tricky. Australia defended well, and their goalkeeper Mark Bosnich made some super saves. It was going to take something very special to beat him. This time, it came from Rui.

As he dribbled infield on his left foot, his opposite number in Australia's midfield followed him all the way. Rui needed to shake him off somehow. So, he faked to shoot and moved the ball to his right foot instead. With an extra yard of space, he smashed the ball into the top corner. 1–0!

'What a strike!' Luís cried out as he jumped on his friend.

Portugal were now just one win away from a second Under-20 World Cup trophy in a row. The whole nation was behind them: 90,000 fans had watched their quarter-final in the stadium, and then 112,000 had watched their semi-final.

Now, for the final, there were 127,000 fans in the Estádio da Luz in Lisbon!

Out on the pitch, Luís looked up and he could barely see the sky above the rows and rows of supporters. It was an amazing sight. Sporting's Alvalade Stadium could only hold 65,000 fans, and that was just for the big Lisbon derby against Benfica. This was a whole different level for Luís and he loved it.

The atmosphere was absolutely incredible. He had never heard noise like this. He was usually so calm and focused before a big game, but even he could feel the goosebumps rising on his skin. As the Portuguese national anthem played, Luís placed his right hand over his heart and sang along. He was so proud to represent his country, and so determined to win the trophy.

The team standing in their way was Brazil. Their strikers Paulo Nunes and Giovane Élber were in great form and their left-back Roberto Carlos loved to get forward and attack. Portugal would have to be very careful.

The crowd cheered every Portugal pass and booed every Brazilian foul. There were plenty of those because everyone was so fired up for the final.

'Ref!' Luís cried out as a player pushed him to the floor.

He got back up and kept looking for ways to unlock the Brazil defence. Portugal tried and tried. João hit the post but that was as close as they got to a goal.

After forty-five minutes, it was 0–0. After ninety minutes, it was still 0–0. After 120 minutes, it was *still* 0–0. The final would be decided by penalties yet again. The tension in the air was almost unbearable.

As Luís sat on the halfway line with his tired teammates, he tried to lift their spirits. 'I know we lost the shoot-out last year in Hungary, but we're a better team now. We're so much stronger. Come on – let's show that we learnt our lesson!'

In the stands above them, the fans waved their

Portuguese flags from side to side. They still believed that their national team would win.

Ramon went first for Brazil and… scored!

Jorge went first for Portugal and… scored!

Élber went next for Brazil and… hit the crossbar!

As Luís walked forward to the penalty spot, he knew that he had a golden chance to put Portugal in the lead. He took his time, placing the ball down in the same careful way that he had tied his boots in front of Aurélio Pereira all those years ago.

Luís took five steps back and waited for the referee's whistle. The goalkeeper dived the right way, but he couldn't reach it. It was a perfectly-placed penalty.

Goooooooooooooooooooooaaaaaaaaaaaaaaaaaaalllllll lllllllllllllllllllllll!!!!!!!!!!!!!!!!!!!

'Yes!' Luís roared, pumping his fist at the fans.

As he jogged past his goalkeeper, he gave him a high-five. 'One save and we've won!'

Andrei scored for Brazil, and Paulo scored for Portugal.

Marquinhos went next for Brazil and… the keeper saved it!

Rui had the chance to win the World Cup for his country. He took a long run-up and… scored!

The players jumped over the advertising boards to celebrate with the supporters. The message was big and bold up on the screen – 'Portugal: World Champions'.

'We did it!' Luís cheered as he hugged Rui.

It was the best moment of their young lives. The Portugal players did a full lap of honour around the pitch, lifting the trophy high above their heads.

Luís had won the World Cup with the Under-20s. Could he now go on and win the World Cup with the Portugal senior team too? He couldn't wait to find out.

CHAPTER 9

SENIOR DEBUT

It didn't take long for Luís to move up from Portugal's Under-20s, after their World Cup win, to the senior team. It was just two months later, and when it came to match day, he wasn't just in the squad; he was in the starting XI. At the age of eighteen, he was about to make his full international debut, in a friendly against Luxembourg.

'Everything's happening so fast!' he told his dad excitedly.

There was a real mix of young and old in the team. Luís lined up with his Under-20 mates Emílio and João but also present were his Sporting captain Pedro Venâncio and even his childhood hero Paulo Futre. It was Portugal past, present *and* future all together.

In childhood, Luís had dreamed of making his international debut at Sporting's Alvalade Stadium in front of 60,000 cheering fans, where he would have dribbled past every opponent to score a winning wondergoal.

However, the reality, when it came, wasn't quite so exciting. Instead, in October 1991, Luís made his international debut at Luxembourg's Municipal Stadium in front of only 3,000 fans. He was so desperate to show off his skills at the top level, but he struggled to get into the game and he was taken off at half-time. It certainly wasn't the best debut of Luís's career.

'Don't worry, you'll have bigger and better games than that!' Pedro said as he joined him on the subs bench.

The match ended in a 1–1 draw. It was a poor result that showed just how far Portugal had fallen. Since the 1986 World Cup, they hadn't qualified for Euro 88 or the 1990 World Cup.

'How are we going to get to another major tournament if we can't even beat Luxembourg?' Emílio moaned on the way back to Lisbon.

Luís tried to focus on the positives. He was now a senior international and, with the Golden Generation, he was going to turn things around for his country.

That couldn't happen straight away, however. Luís was still a teenager and he had only just started playing regularly at club level. International football was another big step-up to get used to.

'There's no rush,' the Portugal manager Carlos Queiroz reassured him. He had moved up from the Under-20s at the same time as Luís, and he wanted to protect his young star. 'I know you can do it, and you know you can do it, but let's take our time to get it right!'

At first, Queiroz kept Luís on the bench in the big games. That was frustrating because it was hard for him to do something special when he only came on for the last few minutes. In the friendly matches, however, Luís got the chance to start and shine. What could he do to show his manager that he was ready to play the full ninety minutes in every match?

In the Stade de France in Paris, in November 1992, Portugal played against Bulgaria. Luís wore the Number 11 shirt with pride. Every time he got the ball on the right wing, he dribbled forward with speed and skill. The only way that the left-back could stop him was by fouling him. As long as he didn't get injured, Luís didn't mind – it was a clear sign that he was winning the battle.

'This is going to be a good day!' he thought to himself.

Portugal won a free kick on the right. Luís wanted to take it but there was a queue of senior players ahead of him.

'Okay, well, wait for me to get into the penalty area, then!' he told his teammates. If he couldn't set up a goal, perhaps he could score one instead.

The cross was brilliant, but Luís's header was even better. He jumped up high, just like he had for his first Sporting goal against Torreense. But that was only the first part of the challenge. Next, Luís's header needed to be powerful *and* accurate. It was both of those things and more. The ball flew into the corner of the net before the goalkeeper could even move his arms.

Gooooooooooooaaaaaaaaalllllllllllllllllllllll!!!!!!!!!!!!

Luís couldn't believe it – he had scored his first goal for his country! It was an amazing feeling to be surrounded by all the other Portugal players. They were celebrating because of him.

'Great work!' his old teammate Oceano cheered.

'Another header!' his friend Emílio laughed. 'What's going on? I thought you were a tricky winger, not a big target man. Did you really mean to do that?'

'Of course!' Luís said, nodding confidently.

Yes, he preferred to beat defenders with his fancy footwork, but he wasn't afraid to get stuck in and fight for his country.

Two months later, in a World Cup qualifier against Malta, Portugal won another free kick on the right. This time, Luís was allowed to take it. His reputation was growing within the team and he now had a year's experience. He curled a really dangerous cross into the six-yard box for Rui Águas to score. 1–0!

On the sideline, Queiroz smiled. With two match-winning performances in a row, Luís had shown that he was now ready to become a national hero.

CHAPTER 10

GOLDEN PLAYER

Luís was so calm and confident on the pitch that he often looked like an old, experienced star. However, he was still young enough to play at the 1994 Under-21 European Championships in France. Portugal's Golden Generation was back together for one last junior tournament – Luís, João, Rui, Paulo, Jorge and the rest. They couldn't wait.

'This is our warm-up for Euro 96!' captain João told his teammates.

Portugal had failed to qualify for the 1994 World Cup, so Euro 96 was Portugal's next big target. The youngsters were ready and raring to help their country get there.

First, however, they had the Under-21 Euros to

win. It was going to be a very tough test of their tremendous talent because they weren't the only country with a new golden generation.

France had Christophe Dugarry, Claude Makélélé and a talented playmaker called Zinedine Zidane. Italy, meanwhile, had Francesco Toldo, Christian Panucci, Fabio Cannavaro, Filippo Inzaghi *and* Christian Vieri.

'Bring it on!' Luís cheered. He loved challenging himself against the very best.

In the quarter-finals, Portugal faced Poland. They were the clear favourites to win but at half-time in the first leg, they were losing 1–0.

Portugal's manager, Nelo Vingada, wasn't happy with his players. 'Do you think you're too good for this?' he asked them angrily. 'Because if you think that, you're wrong. You're only as good as your most recent performance and right now, that's pretty awful!'

With their manager's words ringing in their ears, the Golden Generation bounced back in style. João and Rui scored the goals, but Luís was the star who set them up. He was like a racing car, accelerating into top gear.

Portugal eventually won 5–1 on aggregate and set up a semi-final against Spain. They would have to win without Luís, however. He was suspended, after picking up a yellow card in each game against Poland.

'Bad luck,' Rui said, putting an arm around his disappointed friend. 'At least you'll be back in time to win the final for us!'

Luís smiled but inside, he still felt miserable. There was nothing he hated more than watching his team from the sidelines. It was a nightmare. What if Portugal lost and there was nothing he could do to help? Luckily, Portugal didn't lose. Thanks to Rui and João, they powered through to yet another final.

'I never doubted you guys for a second!' Luís lied. This time, he was smiling for real.

He couldn't wait for the big final against Italy. Luís knew that Portugal's attackers would need to be at their very best to beat Toldo, Panucci and Cannavaro. They had only let in one goal all tournament.

'Hey, but so have we!' Jorge argued. He was always sticking up for the defence. 'We've got nothing to be scared of.'

As soon as the final kicked off, players raced around, flying into tackles and booting the ball up the pitch. That wasn't Luís's style, though. He liked to take his time. After all, you can't rush beautiful football.

'Calm down and think!' Luís told his teammates, tapping his brain.

He played neat passes and looked to create some magic in the middle of the chaos. That was a very difficult task against Italy, the best defenders in the world. Luís did well to escape from his marker, then passed inside and ran forward for the one-two.

Olé!

The Portugal fans clapped and cheered but when he got the ball back, Luís was surrounded by three men in blue. There was nowhere for him to go, and yet he didn't give up. As he dribbled down the right wing, his legs got tangled up with the legs of the left-back.

'Foul!' he screamed as he fell to the floor.

The referee shook his head and waved 'play on'. Luís lay on the grass, holding his left leg and crying out in pain. The physio rushed onto the field.

Everyone looked very worried – the Portugal

coaches, the Portugal players and the Portugal supporters too. Was it serious? Was their star player going to have to go off injured?

No! After some magic spray, Luís got back up and carried on. He had a final to win for his country. He wasn't going to let a few heavy tackles stop him. He moved from the right to the middle to the left and then back again. He was looking for the space to dribble and create.

'All we need is one good chance,' he told Rui, holding up a finger. 'One!'

The two best young teams in Europe were so evenly-matched. As hard as they tried, they just couldn't score against each other. After ninety minutes of football, it was still 0–0.

'Not again!' Luís muttered to himself.

His shoulders slumped. When the pressure was really on, Portugal seemed to get stage fright. First Scotland in 1989, then the Soviet Union in 1990, then Brazil in 1991, and now Italy in 1994. They hadn't scored a single goal in any of those big games. Yet.

'Keep going!' Vingada shouted, patting his star

player on the back. 'Go out there and win it in extra time!'

Luís did his best. Every time he got the ball, he looked for a perfect, defence-splitting pass to João. However, that was like trying to thread a football through the eye of a needle. Impossible!

In the ninety-seventh minute, Italy's Pierluigi Orlandini dribbled infield and fired an unstoppable shot into the top corner. Golden Goal! Portugal's Euro dream was over.

Luís couldn't believe it. He stood with his hands on his hips, staring up at the sky. It was such a heartbreaking way to lose a big final. The Portugal players collapsed onto the grass in shock and misery. They were meant to be the Golden Generation and they had truly believed that they would win.

Luís won the tournament's Golden Player award but it wasn't what he really wanted. After a few days of despair, it was time for them all to look ahead.

'Come on, it's all about Euro 96 now!' he told his teammates.

CHAPTER 11

BARCELONA BOUND

By the age of just twenty-two, Luís was the captain of Sporting Lisbon. He wore the yellow armband with pride and focus. He wasn't 'the next big thing' anymore.

Instead, Luís was an international footballer with three full seasons of league experience. He was the best player in the Portuguese league. He even had a Golden Ball trophy to prove it. As well as creating lots of goals, he was also now scoring them too. Luís felt ready to lead Sporting to glory.

'I'm tired of waiting to win a trophy,' he told Emílio ahead of the 1994–95 season. 'We keep finishing third or fourth and that's not good enough. We need to finish first!'

Sporting's new manager was Carlos Queiroz, Luís's biggest fan. Queiroz had coached him in the Portugal Under-20s and in the senior national team as well. He knew how much talent Luís had and how to get the best out of that talent.

'I'm giving you a free role,' his manager told him. 'Play everywhere – on the right wing, the left wing *and* through the middle. Make the most of those incredible gifts – your skill and vision!'

Luís loved it. He was always on the move, making it really difficult for defenders to mark him. And it was even harder to tackle him. As he dribbled forward, they backed away in fear. Which way would Luís go, right or left? Often, they didn't know until it was too late.

Goooooooooooooooooooooaaaaaaaaaaaaaalllllllllllllll llllllllllllll!!!!!!!!!!!!!!

Luís's match-winning performances were both good news and bad news for Sporting. On the one hand, the team was having a great season. For the first time in years, they were challenging Porto for the league and cup double. But on the other hand,

Europe's biggest clubs now wanted to sign Luís, and they had lots of money to spend.

'Don't go!' Emílio pleaded. 'Not yet anyway. We have to win a trophy together first!'

Luís had a very tough decision to make. Playing in the top leagues was his dream. It was the next step in his football journey, and he knew that he could do it. This was his chance to prove himself at the highest level. However, could he leave Sporting, his first club, in the middle of a season, without giving the fans something to celebrate first?

'Let's just wait and see what offers you get,' his agent suggested.

At the beginning, it was Italian giants Juventus and Parma who battled it out to buy him. Juventus had amazing players like Roberto Baggio, Didier Deschamps and Luís's Portugal teammate Paulo Sousa.

'Come join me!' Paulo tried to persuade Luís. 'You'll enjoy it here.'

But Parma had amazing players too, like Gianfranco Zola, Faustino Asprilla and another of

Luís's Portugal teammates, Fernando Couto.

'Come join me!' Fernando tried to persuade him. 'You'll enjoy it here.'

Both offers were so brilliant that Luís couldn't choose between Juventus and Parma. So, he signed an agreement with both teams and that was a big mistake. In the end, he didn't sign for either of them because he was told that he couldn't sign for an Italian team at all.

Luís was disappointed, but he didn't give up on his dream. 'Do any other big clubs want to buy me?' he asked his agent.

His old Sporting coach Malcolm Allison recommended him to English club Manchester City. 'Figo is going to be a world beater!' he promised them.

Manchester City were very keen to sign Luís, but they couldn't compete with Barcelona, one of the biggest clubs in the world, whose manager – the Dutch legend Johan Cruyff – was looking for a talented young winger to replace Michael Laudrup.

'How can I say no to that!' Luís said immediately,

his eyes wide with excitement.

Sporting couldn't say no either. Barcelona were willing to pay £2 million for Luís and loan him back for the rest of the season.

'That means we can still win a trophy together!' Luís told Emílio happily.

Sadly, the Portuguese League title was now out of reach. Sporting were in second place but a long way behind Porto. It would have to be the Portuguese Cup instead.

Luís was a man on a mission. He scored two goals in the quarter-final against Olivais e Moscavide, and as they headed into the semi-final against Vitória de Setúbal, he wanted to score again more than anything. The game began, and as Krasimir Balakov held the ball up, Luís made a clever late run into the box. The pass was good, but a defender was rushing towards him. He hit the shot first time, with the outside of his left boot. The ball was in the bottom corner before the goalkeeper could even dive.

Goooooooooooooooooooooooooaaaaaaaaaaaaaallllllll llllllllllllllllllll!!!!!!!!!!!!!!!

Luís jumped for joy and pointed up at the supporters. He would never forget them and, by winning the Cup, he was going to make sure that they never forgot him either.

Sporting were on fire. Luís dribbled down the right wing and passed inside to Krasimir, who dummied the ball. It ran through to Emmanuel Amunike, who blasted it into the net. 2–0!

Luís saved the best until last. From just outside the penalty area, he hit a swerving rocket into the top corner.

Goooooooooooooooooooooooaaaaaaaaaaaalllllllllllll llllllllllll!!!!!!!!!!!!!!!!!

With another two goals, Luís was in unstoppable form. This time, he jumped over the advertising boards to celebrate right in front of the fans. With his arms up in the air, he roared, 'Come on!'

In the cup final, Sporting faced Marítimo, the team that Luís had made his club debut against five years earlier. If everything went according to plan, he would be giving the fans the perfect leaving present.

The National Stadium in Lisbon was packed for

the big game. There were lots of Marítimo supporters there too, but the only colours that Luís could see were green and white. The Sporting fans had been waiting a long time for something to cheer about.

The party started after ten minutes, when Ivaylo Yordanov scored his first goal. Seventy-five minutes later, he scored again to seal the victory. It hadn't been Luís's greatest game but that didn't matter. His Sporting team had won their first trophy at last.

'We did it!' he cheered, hugging Emílio.

The atmosphere in the stadium was electric. Luís climbed up on his teammate's shoulders and pumped his fists. He didn't want this incredible moment to ever end. However, after the trophy presentation and a victory lap around the pitch, Luís's Sporting career did indeed end.

It was time for him to move on. He was Barcelona bound.

CHAPTER 12

EURO 96

After the disappointments of Euro 88, the 1990 World Cup, Euro 92 and the 1994 World Cup, Portugal finally qualified for Euro 96. Luís and the Golden Generation made sure that their country didn't miss a fifth major tournament in a row. They beat the Republic of Ireland and Austria to finish top of Group 6. Luís and João scored three goals each along the way, while Rui scored four.

'England, here we come!' they cheered happily together.

Luís couldn't wait. He had played in lots of international competitions before but nothing as big as this. Eight thousand supporters had watched their 1994 Under-21 Euro final in Montpellier, France.

Now, 35,000 supporters were there watching their first Euro 96 match in Sheffield, England. There was so much excitement in the air.

'It's a sell-out, boys!' their manager António Oliveira told them before kick-off.

They were up against Denmark, the reigning Champions of Europe. Peter Schmeichel was in goal and the Laudrup Brothers were in attack. Brian played for Glasgow Rangers, while Michael – by now at Real Madrid – was the winger who Luís had replaced at Barcelona. The Portugal players didn't mind being the underdogs. In fact, they liked it. It meant that they could catch teams by surprise. They weren't there at Euro 96 to make up the numbers; they were there to win matches.

Although Denmark were definitely surprised, Portugal didn't quite get the win they wanted. Luís, Rui and Paulo Sousa had lots of possession in midfield, but they struggled to turn that into goals. Every time they got a good chance to score, either Schmeichel made a top save, or their forwards fluffed it.

'Hey, at least we got a draw,' Rui argued at the final whistle.

'Yes, but we should have won that!' Luís replied, shaking his head.

He was feeling especially frustrated because Oliveira had taken him off with thirty minutes still to go. Luís wanted to play every minute but his legs were tired after playing over fifty matches in his first season at Barcelona. What he really needed was a rest, not a big international tournament. However, he wasn't going to let tired legs get in the way of achieving his dreams.

'On to the next match,' Luís told himself and off he went, back to working hard.

Portugal looked like they were heading for another dominant draw against Turkey, but luckily, Fernando Couto scored a winner. Luís's first feeling was relief but after the match, worry crept in.

'We can't rely on the defenders to get our goals,' he discussed with João. 'We need a top-class finisher!'

Until Portugal found a proper striker, Luís would

do his best to fill the gap. Against Croatia, he sprinted into the box as Secretário raced down the right wing. Secretário's cross landed right in front of him near the penalty spot. Luís was unmarked, with just the goalkeeper to beat. All he had to do was stay calm, and luckily 'Calm' was his middle name. Luís chested the ball down and coolly poked it past the keeper.

Goooooooooooooooooooooooaaaaaaaaaaalllllllllllllll lllllllllllllll!!!!!!!!!!!

Luís ran towards the fans with his right arm up in the air and a big smile across his face. He was off the mark at Euro 96, and his team were heading through to the quarter-finals.

Their quarter-final opponents would be the Czech Republic, the tournament's other surprise package. They had already knocked out Italy in the group stage, so Portugal would have to be careful.

'Trust me, they're a very dangerous team to play against,' Oliveira warned his players. 'If we relax for a second, they'll make us pay!'

In the first half, it was the same old story for

Portugal. They moved the ball nicely from side to side, but they couldn't get past the Czech defence. Even when they did, they then couldn't get past the Czech keeper. The fans were getting restless. They wanted more action, and they wanted goals.

'We need a Plan B,' Luís argued in the dressing room. 'All this passing is getting us nowhere!'

But just as they tried to play more attacking football, the Czech Republic pounced. Out of nowhere, Karel Poborský dribbled straight into the Portuguese penalty area and went to lob the ball over the keeper, Vítor Baía.

From the halfway line, Luís watched Poborský's chip loop up high into the air. It looped up so high that surely it would keep on rising over the crossbar. That's what all of Portugal hoped for. But instead, the ball dropped down into the back of the net. 1–0!

The Portugal players just stood there, stunned. What had just happened? And how had it happened?

'Switch on again!' Oliveira shouted at his players. 'There's plenty of time left!'

But Portugal couldn't score, not even when

the Czech Republic had a player sent off. Luís ran and ran but nothing was working. Why couldn't he create just a little bit of magic? That's all they needed.

With fifteen minutes to go, Luís was substituted. As he trudged off the pitch, he knew that his Euro 96 was over. He felt like he had let his country down, right when they needed him the most.

After a few days of disappointment, however, Luís was able to look on the bright side. He had scored a goal, and Portugal had played well in their first big tournament for ten years. Only a freak goal had knocked them out. The players had lessons to learn, but they could be proud of their performances.

'The World Cup is the one we want to win anyway!' Luís joked. The next one was now less than two years away.

CHAPTER 13

RUNNING RIOT WITH RONALDO I

Back in Barcelona, Luís couldn't wait for his big second season to start. His Portugal teammates Vítor and Fernando had joined him at the club and so had his old Sporting manager, Bobby Robson. It was nice to have so many familiar faces around, but Luís was most excited about one of the new faces. Barcelona had signed a Brazilian striker called Ronaldo from PSV Eindhoven.

'Have you watched any videos of his best goals?' Luís asked Fernando. 'Wow, he looks incredible!'

Fernando wasn't so sure. 'Those goals were in the Dutch League, though. Let's wait and see if he can score like that in Spain!'

In training, it was soon Fernando vs Ronaldo, the new defender against the new attacker. Who would win? As the battle began, Ronaldo had an important advantage – Luís was on his team. Again and again, he dribbled down the right wing, looking for a clever pass to his new Brazilian teammate. After twisting one way and then the other, Luís played the ball into Ronaldo's path.

Fernando thought he could deal with the danger. If he marked his opponent tightly, how could he escape? With a nutmeg! In a flash, Ronaldo flicked the ball through Fernando's legs and burst into the box. He was so fast that no-one could catch up with him.

Luís had stopped running. He was a spectator, watching an amazing show of skill. Ronaldo just had Vítor left to beat. He faked to shoot one way but as the keeper dived at his feet, he turned the other way. Ronaldo's finale was a pass into the empty goal.

Vítor and Fernando looked even more shocked than when Poborský scored the lob against them at Euro 96.

'Okay, you're right,' Fernando admitted afterwards. 'He *is* incredible!'

Luís laughed. 'I'm not sure he was even trying that hard today. Imagine what he can do in a real match!'

On his debut in the Spanish Super Cup Final against Atlético Madrid, Ronaldo dribbled through three defenders and fired the ball into the bottom corner. 1–0! He made it look so easy.

Playing with such a superstar, Luís had to up his game. He moved over to the left wing, beat the right-back and delivered a perfect cross for Giovanni. 2–0!

At the final whistle, the whole team celebrated a huge 5–2 victory.

'We're going to have a lot of fun together this season!' Luís told Ronaldo with a smile.

Barcelona's top trophy target was the Spanish League title. To win it, they would have to beat their massive rivals Real Madrid, as well as Valencia, Deportivo de La Coruña and Atlético Madrid. With Ronaldo and Luís running riot, however, anything was possible.

The 1996–97 season soon became a thrilling two-horse race between Barcelona and Real Madrid. Barcelona had the better attackers, but Real Madrid had the better defenders. There were big battles all over the pitch, but the biggest of all was Luís's battle against Real's left-back, Roberto Carlos. Both players had so much skill, speed and determination. There could only be one winner.

That was Roberto Carlos in the first 'El Clásico' match, as Real Madrid claimed a 2–0 victory. They managed to keep Luís and Ronaldo quiet all night. For the return match at the Nou Camp, the Barcelona players were really fired up. They needed a win and they needed revenge. There were six games left in the season, and the title race was still on.

With 90,000 fans cheering him on, Luís attacked at full speed. Roberto Carlos backed away, waiting for the right moment. Would Luís dribble down the wing with his right foot or cut inside on his left? He always kept defenders guessing. Luís fooled Roberto Carlos with a brilliant stepover and cut inside on his left foot. As he burst into the box, Roberto Carlos panicked and slid in from behind. Penalty!

Ronaldo's spot-kick was saved but the rebound fell to Luís. He calmly crossed the ball back to Ronaldo for an easy finish. 1–0!

'Thanks, what a hero!' the Brazilian cheered, high-fiving Luís.

In the end, however, even that win wasn't enough. Real Madrid won the Spanish League title by just two points. For Barcelona, it felt like a failure but at least it wasn't the only trophy that they were fighting for. They had already won the UEFA Cup Winners' Cup Final against PSG and they were into the Spanish Cup Final against Real Betis.

'Come on, let's do the double!' Luís told his teammates.

They would have to do it without their star striker, however. After winning the FIFA World Player of the Year award for his forty-seven goals in forty-nine games, Ronaldo was off to Inter Milan. It was a big blow for Barcelona but at least they still had Luís. At Real Madrid's Bernabéu Stadium, it was his time to shine.

In the last seconds of the first half, Luís dribbled left and then right. He was looking for space and suddenly he found it on the edge of the Betis box. He was slightly off balance as he kicked it but Luís still managed to curl the ball past the goalkeeper.

Goooooooooooooaaaaaaaaallllllllllllllllllllll!!!!!!!!!!!

Score: 1–1! In the excitement, Luís lifted his shirt over his head and stretched his arms out wide like an aeroplane. He had created a moment of pure magic when his team needed it most.

'What a beauty!' screamed the Barcelona captain, Pep Guardiola. 'Who needs Ronaldo?'

Luís wasn't done yet. In extra time, he skipped past one tackle and raced into the penalty area. He was so determined to be the matchwinner. Luís passed to Juan Antonio Pizzi, who passed to Emmanuel Amuneke. His cross bounced off a defender, then the goalkeeper and landed right in front of Luís. What a stroke of luck!

Goooooooooooooaaaaaaaaallllllllllllllllllllll!!!!!!!!!!!

Luís grabbed the ball from the net, kissed it and lifted it high into the air. The Barcelona fans cheered their hero's name again and again.

Figo! Figo! Figo!

It was a final, and a season, that Luís would never, ever forget.

CHAPTER 14

RUNNING RIOT WITH RIVALDO

The good times didn't stop there for Luís and Barcelona. In fact, that was only the start. No, they didn't have Ronaldo anymore, but the club signed two new Brazilian forwards to replace him. Sonny Anderson had scored lots of goals in the French league with Monaco, while Rivaldo had taken the Spanish league by storm with Deportivo de La Coruña.

With Rivaldo on the left and Sonny through the middle, Barcelona's new star strikeforce was nearly complete. All they needed now was a world-class winger to play on the right. Oh wait, they already had one of those – Luís!

'Come on, we've got trophies to win!' he cheered excitedly.

When Pep got injured, Luís became the new Barcelona captain. He took his role very seriously. It was a huge honour to wear the famous yellow-and-red stripes around his arm. The fans expected a lot from their leader but that was okay because Luís expected a lot from himself, and from his teammates. If they worked together, they could beat Real Madrid and win the La Liga title.

By the time Barcelona travelled to Real Madrid's Bernabéu stadium for the first *El Clásico* of the 1997–98 season, they were already seven points ahead of their rivals. But they could not be complacent.

'We can't relax for a second,' Luís said sternly in the dressing room before kick-off. He was even more fired up than normal. 'If we do, Real will destroy us!'

It was Luís vs Roberto Carlos yet again. Who would win the big battle this time? In the fifth minute of the match, Luís raced down the right wing, with Roberto Carlos trailing behind him. The

Barcelona supporters jumped up out of their seats, ready to celebrate. They had seen Luís do this so many times before.

He looked up and saw Rivaldo making a great run between the centre-backs. The pass would have to be perfect to reach him but if anyone could get it right, it was Luís. Goal!

Rivaldo ran straight to Luís with his arms out ready for the hug. 'What a cross!' he screamed.

But early in the second half, Roberto Carlos crossed and Raúl scored. It was Real Madrid 1 Barcelona 1, and Roberto Carlos 1 Luís 1. Both sets of fans cried out for a winning goal.

With ten minutes to go, Luís raced down the left wing, with Roberto Carlos chasing him once more. The Barcelona supporters jumped up out of their seats again, ready to celebrate. Luís looked up and this time, he saw Giovanni sprinting into the box. Goal!

Giovanni ran straight to Luís with his arms out ready for the hug. 'What a cross!' he screamed.

Luís turned to face the Barcelona fans and pumped

his fists. He was leading the team towards glory, one incredible cross at a time.

In the second *El Clásico* at the Nou Camp, Luís chested the ball down and dribbled at Roberto Carlos. Which way would he go, right or left? With a burst of pace, Luís cut inside on his left foot and curled a beautiful shot into the far corner of the net. The goalkeeper had no chance.

Goooooooooooooooooooooooaaaaaaaaaaaalllllllllllllll llllllllll!!!!!!!!!!!!!!!!!!!!

Luís charged towards the touchline like a raging bull. The amazing atmosphere in the stadium only added to his excitement. 'Come on!' he roared, punching the air with delight.

After doing the double over Real Madrid, Barcelona stormed all the way to the La Liga and Spanish Cup Double. After finishing second or third so many times before, Luís had finally won his first-ever league title. It was the happiest moment of his life.

The celebrations at the Nou Camp were wild. The players jumped into the crowd to join the joyful fans. They returned to the pitch with all kinds of gifts, including scarves, flags and inflatable lollipops. Midfielder Iván de la Peña even drove a cart onto the grass, carrying the rest of the team. They sang and sang until they lost their voices.

Campiones, Campiones, Olé, Olé, Olé!

The next season, Barcelona won the league again. What's more, they finished a massive eleven points ahead of Real Madrid.

'They can't even get close to us!' Pep joked.

Luís celebrated by dying his hair in the club's colours – red and blue. He tried to get Rivaldo to join him, but the Brazilian took one look and laughed. 'No way, mate!'

Barca's deadly duo was now joined by a new third musketeer – Dutch striker Patrick Kluivert. Together, they could not stop scoring. It was an awesome attack, simply unstoppable. Between the three of them, they had way too much pace, power and skill for the Spanish defences. Luís was the most skilful of all.

'Why can't someone just tackle him?!' goalkeepers

shouted when he danced through and scored.

Luís never looked like he was moving that fast, and yet it was so hard to get the ball off him. Luís was the deadliest dribbler around, with perfect balance, close control and two quick feet. He drove defenders crazy.

'It's impossible!' they shouted back at their goalkeepers, kicking the air in frustration.

Luís was loving life in Spain. He was a favourite of fans at Barcelona, one of the biggest football clubs in the world. He had amazing teammates and a growing collection of winners' medals. What was not to love about that?

However, Luís's home country was never far from his mind. His heart would always lie back in Portugal. There was so much he wanted to achieve with the national team. Despite the experience of Euro 96, they didn't make it to the 1998 World Cup in France. There was no shame in finishing behind Germany in qualifying, but behind the Ukraine too? Portugal were better than that.

Luís was devastated to miss out on such a

major tournament. Almost all of his Barcelona teammates were there, playing for Spain, Brazil, the Netherlands, even Bulgaria. Luís was jealous of every single one of them.

'We can't let this happen again,' he told Vítor and Fernando firmly. 'No excuses – Portugal *have* to play at World Cup 2002!'

CHAPTER 15

EURO 2000

Before that next World Cup, however, Portugal had Euro 2000 to focus on. Not only did they qualify, but they did so in style; they thrashed Azerbaijan 7–0 and then Liechtenstein 8–0.

'Finally, we're scoring goals!' Luís joked.

That had been Portugal's problem for years. They created lots and lots of chances, but they couldn't get the ball in the net. Now, however, things were looking up. João and Sá Pinto were scoring more than ever and there were two new strikers on the block – Pauleta and Nuno Gomes.

'I've got a good feeling about this tournament,' Luís told Rui as the team travelled to the Netherlands.

Luís was scoring more than ever too. The 1999–

2000 season had been his best at Barcelona, with
fourteen goals in all competitions. It was time for him
to find the same form for his country. In Portugal's
new 4-3-3 formation, he was on the frontline with
João and Nuno. Luís wasn't a midfielder anymore –
he was an attacker.

Portugal's first game in the Euro 2000
championship was against England. It was a mouth-
watering match-up – Fernando, Luís, Rui and João
vs Sol Campbell, David Beckham, Paul Scholes and
Michael Owen. Who would come out on top?

After twenty minutes, England were 2–0 up. It
was an awful start for Portugal, but the players didn't
panic. They knew they had the quality to fight back.
They just needed to stay strong and believe.

'Come on, they think they've won this already,'
Luís told his teammates. 'Let's show them that's
not true!'

Luís took control of the game. As he dribbled
forward from midfield, the England players
backed away in fear. He was a long way from goal,
surrounded by defenders, and his team were losing.

What did Luís have to lose? Portugal needed their superstar more than ever.

Luís pulled his right leg back and kicked the ball as hard as he could. It flew, straight as an arrow, into the top corner. England's goalkeeper David Seaman didn't even move.

Goooooooooooaaaaaaaaaaaaaaaallllllllllllllllllllllll llll!!!!!!!!!!!!!!!!!!!!!

Luís grabbed the ball and ran back for the restart. He gave a few high-fives along the way but there wasn't time to celebrate his wonderstrike. They had more goals to score.

After that, Portugal really got going. When they raised their game, England looked helpless. Rui crossed and João scored with a brilliant header. 2–2! Rui threaded a through-ball to Nuno and he smashed it in. 3–2!

This time, the players did celebrate. 'What a comeback!' Luís screamed in the middle of the big team hug. At the final whistle, he raised his arms up in the air.

'Well played,' Beckham said as they swapped

shirts, 'and what a goal!'

It was a massive victory that would give Portugal so much confidence. They had shown that at their best, they could beat anyone. With victories over Romania and Germany, they were through to the quarter-finals.

Their manager Humberto Coelho was full of praise. 'That was the "Group of Death" and we won it – well done, everyone!'

Luís wasn't getting carried away, though. In knock-out football, anything could happen. They had learnt that the hard way at Euro 96, with that freak Poborský lob. On paper, Portugal were a better team than Turkey, but they had to show it on the pitch.

'Let's go out there and get the job done,' captain Vítor said in the dressing room. 'I want one hundred per cent effort, right from the kick-off!'

Luís listened to his goalkeeper. In the first half, he was electric and everywhere. He got the ball on the right, he got the ball on the left and sometimes in the middle too.

Luís crossed towards Nuno… the striker stretched

but he couldn't quite reach it!

Luís curled a corner to Costinha at the back post…
Turkey's goalkeeper made a great save!

Luís dribbled past two defenders with ease and hit a
fierce, long-range strike… it went just wide of the post!

Portugal's magician didn't give up. Rui flicked the
ball wide to Luís and he delivered another dangerous
cross into the box. It went over the defender and then
bounced up in front of Nuno. His header skipped
across the grass and into the bottom corner. 1–0!

Finally! The 30,000 Portugal fans in the
Amsterdam Arena went wild, and so did the players.
It was a real relief to score before half-time.

'What a fantastic finish!' Luís cheered as he ran
over to Nuno.

In the second half, they combined again. Luís
twisted and turned, tormenting Turkey's left-back.
The poor defender had no chance. Luís ran into the
penalty area and calmly passed across to Nuno for a
simple tap-in. 2–0!

This time, Nuno ran over to Luís to celebrate.
'You're on fire!' he cheered.

It was true. With his man-of-the-match performances, Luís was becoming one of the stars of Euro 2000. In the semi-final, he was up against one of the tournament's other stars – France's Zinedine Zidane.

'That guy's a genius!' Nuno said, full of admiration.

No-one could argue with that, but Portugal had a gameplan: 'Keep Zizou quiet and get the ball to Luís!'

For fifty minutes, the plan worked perfectly. Their midfielders marked Zidane closely and Nuno scored an excellent goal.

'Keep up the amazing work!' Coelho urged his players at half-time. They were so close to reaching the final.

In the second half, however, France got better and better. Luís did his best to create a second goal for Portugal, but it was Thierry Henry who scored next. 1–1!

The race was on to be the matchwinner. Who would it be, Luís or Zidane?

Luís raced down the left wing and crossed towards Nuno... but Bixente Lizarazu got back to clear it!

Zidane's corner was right in the danger zone… but Marcel Desailly headed wide!

Zidane turned beautifully in the box and passed to Sylvian Wiltord… but he slipped and missed it!

Luís's free kick landed on Abel Xavier's head… but Fabien Barthez tipped it over the bar!

It was an exciting battle between the best players in Europe. However, there could only be one matchwinner. Right at the end of extra time, a shot hit Abel on the arm. The linesman raised his flag and the referee pointed to the spot. Penalty!

The Portugal players were furious. Luís took his shirt off and threw it to the ground. 'It was accidental!' he cried out. 'Do you really think that he handballed that on purpose?'

Zidane stepped up and sent Vítor the wrong way. 2–1 to France!

The semi-final was over, and Portugal were out of Euro 2000. Luís felt robbed but he refused to watch the replays. It didn't matter – what was done was done. Euro 2000 was in the past and Portugal had to move on. It was all about the 2002 World Cup now.

CHAPTER 16

MOVING TO MADRID

The Barcelona fans really loved their players. The club's motto was 'More than just a club', and the team's players were more than just players. They were more than just normal heroes too. They were superheroes.

The players' names were sung loudly in the stadium and worn on the backs of thousands of football shirts. The Barcelona players could do anything, anything except for one thing – sign for their rivals, Real Madrid. That was unforgivable.

Luís was one of Barcelona's most popular players, along with Rivaldo and club captain Pep Guardiola. After five successful seasons at the Nou Camp, Luís wasn't seen as a foreigner anymore. With his winning combination of skill and spirit, the fans treated him like one of their own. They called him 'El Rey León' – 'The Lion King'.

Not everyone at Barcelona was treating Luís like 'The Lion King', however. Although he was one of the team's big stars, he wasn't earning as much money as the others. Luís was frustrated because he always gave everything for the team. Thanks to his amazing performances at Euro 2000, he was now one of the best players in the world. He believed that he deserved a pay rise, but the Barcelona club president, Josep Lluís Núñez, disagreed.

'Fine, I'll go to another club that really appreciates me,' Luís replied in anger.

At that time, Florentino Pérez was looking to become the new club president of Real Madrid. In order to win the race, he needed to promise to make a big new signing for the club. Luís would be the perfect player, but would he be brave enough to make the move from Barcelona to Real? There was only one way to find out. Pérez spoke to Paulo Futre, Luís's childhood hero, and arranged a meeting.

'I want to build a new golden era here at Real,'
Pérez told Luís. 'La Liga, the Spanish Cup, the
Champions League – we're going to win them all.
We already have some great footballers but what we
need is superstars. Superstars like you. I want you to
be our very first Galáctico!'

Luís listened carefully. It was a very tempting
offer. At Barcelona, he had won La Liga twice and
the Spanish Cup twice, but never the Champions
League. In 2000, they had been knocked out in
the semi-finals by Valencia. And who had won the
tournament? Real Madrid! Luís was desperate to win
the top European title.

'Okay, if you become the President,' he agreed
eventually, 'I'll sign for Real Madrid!'

On 16 July 2000, Pérez became the new president
of Real Madrid. Luís had made a promise and now he
had to keep it. Barcelona tried their best to persuade
him to stay but the deal was already done. His old
teammates were shocked and devastated.

'I'm sorry,' was all Luís could say to Rivaldo and
Pep. He hadn't wanted to leave Barcelona on such

bad terms, but football was football.

A week later, Luís stood at the Bernabéu, holding up a white Real shirt with '10 FIGO' on the back. At £37 million, he was now the world's most expensive footballer. It was a lot of pressure to live up to, but he couldn't wait to get started on his new adventure. His new teammates couldn't wait either.

'Welcome!' Roberto Carlos said with a massive grin. 'Finally, we get to play on the same team together. I always hated playing against you!'

Luís was excited about his role in the Real Madrid line-up. He would be playing on the right wing, with Michel Salgado behind him at right-back. Together, they would need to create lots of chances for the strikers, Raúl (González) and Fernando Morientes.

'Let's do this!' Luís cheered.

He was determined to get off to a good start in Madrid. In his first La Liga match against Valencia that September, it was 1–1 with five minutes to go. Sávio's cross from the left landed at Luís's feet. He coolly chipped the ball over the diving keeper and into the net.

Goooooooooooooooooooaaaaaaaaaaaaaaaaalllllllllll llllllllllllllllllll!!!!!!!!!!!!!

Luís threw his arms up in the air. What a start! 70,000 fans cheered his name.

'They love you already!' Raúl said with a smile.

After five games, Real Madrid were top with eleven points, two ahead of Barcelona. Then it was time for the match that everyone had been waiting for – Barcelona vs Real Madrid. Everyone, that is, apart from Luís. He tried to prepare like it was just a normal game, but it wasn't. Luís was really not looking forward to his nightmare return to the Nou Camp.

'One hundred thousand fans shouting horrible abuse at me – I can't wait!' he joked sarcastically with Michel, but inside, he was seriously worried.

The Real Madrid manager Vicente del Bosque was worried too. 'Are you sure you want to play in this game?' he asked.

Luís nodded. 'I made a decision and I have to live with it. I never hide away, and I'm not going to start hiding away now!'

The atmosphere, however, was even worse than

he had expected. To the betrayed Barcelona fans, Luís wasn't 'The Lion King' anymore. He was now 'The Traitor'. To show their anger, they set fire to pictures of him in the Real Madrid kit. There were hurtful banners everywhere and the noise was deafening. As Luís walked out onto the pitch, he had to put his fingers in his ears.

'Are you okay?' Michel asked him.

'Let's just get this over with,' he replied, bravely.

Every time Luís touched the ball, the whole crowd booed. Every time a Barcelona player fouled him, they cheered. When it came to corners, Pedro Munitis grabbed the ball.

'Let me take them today,' said Pedro. 'It's not safe for you to be that close to the fans.'

Real Madrid lost 2–0 but at least Luís's Barcelona return was over. At the final whistle, he hugged old teammates like Sergi, Abelardo and Rivaldo.

'I bet you want to come back after that defeat!' Rivaldo teased him.

Luís looked up at the angry supporters. 'I don't think they'd let me, even if I wanted to!'

CHAPTER 17

BALLON D'OR

Figo! Figo! Figo!

The Real Madrid fans made lots of noise for their first Galáctico as Luís walked out onto the pitch.

He wasn't out there to fly down the right wing. Not yet, anyway. First, he had a trophy to collect. As he looked around the Bernabéu stadium, he saw a sea of gold to celebrate the special occasion.

'The winner of the 2000 Ballon d'Or,' a voice announced, 'LUÍS FIGO!'

The crowd cheered even louder. Luís collected the golden ball and lifted it high into the sky. It was one of his proudest moments, perhaps even the proudest. He had won many team trophies before, as well as the Golden Ball award in Portugal. This, however, was the greatest individual prize in the whole of football. Luís was officially the best player in the world.

'Thank you, thank you!' he said, waving to the fans. He was the first Portuguese player to win it since his dad's hero, Eusébio.

What a year it had been for Luís, full of delight and pain. First, getting to the semi-finals of Euro 2000 with Portugal, and then making the massive move from Barcelona to Real Madrid. Above all, however, it had been yet another year of skilful set-ups and gorgeous goals. Whoever he was playing for or with, Luís was always Mr Reliable.

After lots of photos and clapping, he walked back down the tunnel. He had a football match to play against Real Oviedo, and another league title to win.

'Right, let's do this!' Luís cheered.

After fifteen minutes, Fernando Morientes won the ball and dribbled down the left wing. Luís sprinted into the penalty area to meet the cross.

Goooooooooooooooaaaaaaaaaaaaallllllllllllllllllllllllll llllll!!!!!!!!!!!!!!!!!!!!!!!!!!

He ran to Fernando with his arms out wide. 'Thanks for making my day even better!'

Whenever Real Madrid needed a calm head to save the day, Luís was always there to help. Against Numancia, he dribbled in field and just as he was about to shoot, a defender tripped him. Free kick!

Roberto Carlos ran over to take it but Luís grabbed the ball and didn't let go. 'I've got this,' he said confidently.

After a one step run-up, Luís curled his shot over the wall and into the top corner.

Goooooooooooooooooooooaaaaaaaaaaaaaaaalllllllllllllll llllllllllll!!!!!!!!!!!!!!!!!!

He jumped for joy as he ran over to celebrate with the fans. Roberto Carlos was the first to hug him. 'Not bad. Not bad at all!' he cheered.

'I told you!' Luís said, raising an eyebrow.

Roberto Carlos shrugged. 'That was just beginner's luck. Trust me – you won't be taking the next one!'

By May 2001, Real Madrid were still top of La Liga and through to the semi-finals of the Champions League. Luís was enjoying another successful season.

'It looks like I made the right decision!' he joked with Michel.

Bayern Munich wouldn't be easy opponents, however. They had got to the final in 1999 and the semi-finals in 2000.

'We beat them that time,' Raúl told Luís, 'so they'll be out for revenge.'

At home in the Bernabéu, Real Madrid created chance after chance, but they could not score. Bayern could, though, and they left Spain with a 1–0 lead. It was a frustrating result but Luís didn't let it get him down.

'Right, we've got work to do in Germany,' he declared. There was no way that he was giving up yet.

Even when Bayern took the lead in the Olympiastadion, Luís didn't give up. Instead, he tried to make more magical things happen for his team.

Roberto Carlos played a long ball forward to Raúl. The Spanish striker controlled it perfectly and waited for support. Luís was alert and at his side in a flash.

Raúl rolled the ball across to him and he swept it past Oliver Kahn.

Gooooooooooooooaaaaaaaaaaaaaaaaaalllllllllllllllllll llllllll!!!!!!!!!!!!!!!!!

Luís lifted his arms up and roared. 'Come on, we're still in this!' he told his teammates.

Unfortunately, before Real Madrid could score a second goal, Bayern scored their third. It looked like game over and yet Luís still didn't give up. He kept battling to win the ball and create chances. There was enough time left to save the day, he was sure of it. He took a powerful shot from the right side of the penalty area but this time, Kahn saved it.

Figo! Figo! Figo!

The Real Madrid fans loved his drive and determination. No other world-class winger worked so hard for his team. He only stopped running when the referee blew the final whistle.

Luís was disappointed to lose another Champions League semi-final but his first season at Real Madrid was far from a disaster. He finished with fourteen goals, lots of assists, and a third Spanish League title.

'We're only just getting started!' he told Michel. Luís's Champions League dream would just have to wait for another year, but his ambition still burned as bright as ever.

CHAPTER 18

GALÁCTICOS ARE GO!

Pérez had promised a new golden era at Real Madrid. The club president had also promised Luís that he wouldn't be their only new superstar. In the summer of 2001, Real broke the world transfer record again, signing Zinedine Zidane from Juventus for £46 million.

'I guess the Galácticos Are Go!' Luís told Roberto Carlos excitedly.

Luís had known about Zinedine ever since the Under-21 Euros in 1994. Portugal and France didn't play each other at that tournament but Luís watched him play and saw his amazing talent. They had a similar elegant style with the ball at their feet. When they played, time slowed down, and space opened up in front of them.

'You and Zizou on the same team?' Roberto Carlos replied. 'It's going to be ridiculous!'

Luís and Zinedine had only played against each other once, in the Euro 2000 semi-final between Portugal and France. It had been a brilliant battle that day but now, they would be playing together in the white shirts of Real Madrid.

Right from the beginning, Luís and Zinedine had a crazy connection on the pitch. They both always knew where each other would be for the flick, pass or one-two. It was beautiful to watch but it wasn't just the two of them. The whole team was playing entertaining football.

Against Espanyol, Roberto Carlos passed to Raúl, who laid the ball to Zinedine for the shot. 1–0!

Real Madrid won a free kick. Zinedine rolled it across to Luís, who stopped it dead for Roberto Carlos to strike. 2–0!

Zinedine passed to Roberto Carlos, who passed to Luís. Luís tried to flick the ball round the defender but he was fouled. Penalty – 3–0!

Raúl played a lovely one-two with Pedro Munitis. 4–1!

Luís passed to Raúl who played a through-ball to Michel. Michel crossed for Steve McManaman. 5–1!

At their best, Real Madrid were absolutely unstoppable.

'Now we just need to play like that in the Champions League!' Luís told Zinedine. That was the big target for the 2001–02 season.

In the quarter-finals, Real Madrid played Bayern Munich again. Luís rubbed his hands with glee. He was going to make sure that revenge tasted as sweet as honey. Real lost the first leg 2–1 but they had an important away goal to take back to the Bernabéu.

'It's time to turn on the style!' Vicente del Bosque told his players in the dressing room.

Luís and Zinedine created chance after chance but not one of them ended up in the Bayern net. The Real Madrid fans were starting to worry. A draw wasn't good enough. They needed goals. In the second half, Iván Helguera eventually scored from

Roberto Carlos's cross. The whole team celebrated in a heap on the grass.

'Finally!' Luís cheered, breathing a sigh of relief.

Things didn't get any easier for Real Madrid in the semi-finals. They were up against their Spanish rivals, Barcelona. It was time for two extra editions of El Clásico. Luís wasn't too upset that he was suspended for the first leg at the Nou Camp.

His last trip in the league had been terrible. Every time Luís took a corner, fans threw things at him – coins, bottles, even a pig's head. The match had to be stopped for twenty minutes, so that the officials could clear everything off the pitch. It was an awful experience but Luís had to grin and bear it. Sadly, the Barca supporters would never forgive him for joining the enemy, Real Madrid.

'Come closer!' Luís shouted to Michel.

He wanted to play it short but the right-back refused. It was a danger zone down there. 'No way, you're on your own, mate!' Michel called back.

This time, his Real Madrid teammates would have to face the scary atmosphere without him.

'Show no fear!' Luís told them in the tunnel. If he could be brave against Barcelona, then so could the rest of them.

Thanks to goals from Zinedine and Steve, Real Madrid left the Nou Camp with a 2–0 lead. Luís was delighted but he knew that the tie wasn't over yet.

'Focus until the final whistle!' was del Bosque's pre-game message at the Bernabéu.

The players didn't let their manager down. With a 1–1 draw, Real Madrid knocked out Barcelona.

'We're into the final!' Luís cheered, hugging their goalscoring hero, Raúl.

For the Champions League Final, Glasgow's Hampden Park was packed with over 50,000 singing supporters. It was the biggest match of the European season, after all. On the pitch, Luís and his Real Madrid teammates shook hands with their opponents, Bayer Leverkusen.

Real were the big favourites to win but they couldn't underestimate Leverkusen. The Germans had already beaten Juventus, Liverpool *and* Manchester United. Would Real beat them next?

'Come on, let's play like we played against Barcelona!' the captain Fernando Hierro called out.

They got off to a brilliant start. Raúl raced after Roberto Carlos's long throw and caught the goalkeeper by surprise. 1–0! The final wasn't even ten minutes old.

'I didn't know you could run that fast!' Luís joked with Raúl as they shared a celebration hug. 'You really want to win your third trophy, don't you? Almost as much as I want to win my first!'

Five minutes later, however, Lúcio made it 1–1. The Real Madrid players threw their arms up in frustration. 'Come on, we can't throw this away!' Fernando Hierro shouted.

They had some defending to do, and that meant everyone, even their Galácticos. Luís chased back to stop the Leverkusen left-back. He didn't mind doing the dirty work. He wasn't having one of his best games in attack, but that could change in an instant. Iván nearly scored from one of his trademark crosses.

'More of those please!' he shouted to Luís.

Seconds before half-time, Roberto Carlos flicked a high ball to Zinedine on the edge of the penalty area. As it fell from the sky, Zinedine swivelled his body and watched the ball carefully onto his left foot. He caught it perfectly and the volley flew into the top corner.

Goooooooooooooooooooooooaaaaaaaaaaaaaalllllllll llllllllllllllllllllll!!!!!!!!!!!!!!!!

Zinedine sprinted over to the corner flag, with his teammates trailing behind. Luís was one of the first to congratulate him.

'You're a genius!' he cheered.

After sixty minutes, del Bosque brought Luís off. He was a little disappointed with his own performance but if the team won, that was all that really mattered.

'Good luck!' he said to his replacement, Steve.

Luís spent the last thirty minutes of the game watching anxiously from the bench. At the final whistle, he ran back onto the pitch to celebrate. Real Madrid were the Champions of Europe!

'We did it!' Luís told Raúl as they jumped up and

down together with their winners' medals around their necks.

When Fernando Hierro lifted the trophy, shoots of fire rose from the stadium roof and music filled the air:

> *We are the champions, my friends,*
> *And we'll keep on fighting 'til the end.*

Luís sang along with tears of joy in his eyes. It was another proud moment in his amazing career. The Spanish League, the Spanish Cup and now the Champions League – Luís had won them all. What was there left to win?

The World Cup!

CHAPTER 19

WORLD CUP 2002

As Luís stepped off the plane in South Korea, he smiled. At the age of twenty-nine, he was finally about to play in his first World Cup. The experience was everything that he had expected and more.

For one month, football took over not just South Korea and Japan, where the tournament was being held, but the whole wide world. Thirty-two nations were involved, from all over Europe, Asia, Africa, North America, South America and Australia. Fans had travelled thousands of miles to cheer for their countries. With all the colours and sounds, it felt more like a festival than a tournament. It was the greatest football festival ever and this time, Luís and Portugal were taking part.

It was a dream come true for Luís, but his dreams didn't end there. He wanted to do more than just play in a World Cup. He wanted to go all the way and win it.

'It's not too late for our Golden Generation,' he told Rui. 'We're in our prime!'

Luís had scored six goals in qualification and he was looking to score lots more at the actual tournament. In Group D, Portugal were up against the USA, Poland and co-hosts South Korea. There were high hopes of reaching at least the second round.

'One win at a time,' the manager António Oliveira warned his players cautiously. 'We don't want a repeat of that England match at Euro 2000.'

In actual fact, though, Portugal's opening World Cup match was even worse. Against England, Portugal had been 2–0 down, but they fought back to win 3–2. Against the USA in 2002, Portugal were 3–0 down when their fightback began. Luís curled a corner to the back post and Beto scored. 3–1!

'Come on, we can still turn this around!' Luís

urged his teammates. He had waited so long for the chance to play at a World Cup and he was determined to make it last as long as possible.

Portugal managed to pull it back to 3–2 but that was how the match finished. It was a nightmare start. There was no time for self-pity, however. They still had two more group games and with two wins, they could still make it through.

'Go out there and take out your frustrations on Poland!' Oliveira told them.

Looking up at all of the Portugal flags flying around the Jeonju World Cup Stadium, Luís took a deep breath and focused on the next ninety minutes. They couldn't let their nation down again.

João played a great pass to Pauleta. He controlled the ball and then found the bottom corner. 1–0!

Luís made a great run down the right wing. As the ball arrived, he was already thinking one step ahead. That's what world-class players did. Luís whipped a fizzing, first-time cross into the six-yard box for Pauleta. 2–0!

Rui threaded a through-ball to Pauleta. He turned

one way, then the other, and then shot past the keeper. 3–0!

In the stands, the Portuguese tambourines were making plenty of noise. The USA defeat was in the past. Now, against Poland, Pauleta was their hat-trick hero, but the win was a big team effort.

'Thanks guys,' said Pauleta, hugging João, Luís and Rui at the final whistle. 'I couldn't have done it without you!'

Luís was pleased to get his first World Cup win. It was a step in the right direction, towards that World Cup Final. Next step – beating South Korea.

'They'll have the home crowd behind them tonight,' the team captain Fernando Couto reminded the players. 'That's a big advantage but we're the better team. Don't forget that. Let's go knock them out of their own World Cup!'

As the Portuguese national anthem played, Luís closed his eyes and focused on the task ahead. He was desperate to be the hero and make his country proud. As the anthem ended, the fans roared, and the players clapped. It was time for kick-off.

Some of the Portugal players seemed nervous
– but not Luís. He passed the ball around calmly,
waiting patiently for the space to dribble. Before he
found that space, however, João lunged in for a bad
tackle on a South Korean player. He put his hands
up to say sorry, expecting to get a telling off or maybe
a yellow card. But instead, the referee showed him
a red!

'No way!' Luís complained with all his teammates.
'You can't send him off for that!'

But the referee wasn't going to change his mind.
Portugal were down to ten men and halfway through
the second half, they lost another player. To make
matters even worse, South Korea then took the lead.

It was a total tragedy. Luís was furious but it was
goals, not anger, which would help his team to
fight back and win. He was meant to be Portugal's
superstar and one of the best players in the world.
Now was the time to prove it. Soon he got a free kick
on the edge of the area. He curled the ball up over
the wall, past the diving goalkeeper, but just wide of
the post.

'So close!' Luís screamed, putting his hands to his face. Would he get a better chance to score?

No, but his teammates would. Fernando Couto's header bounced down in front of Nuno in the six-yard box. He only had the keeper to beat, but the ball got trapped under his feet.

Sérgio Conceição's strike did beat the keeper, but it bounced off the post and away from danger.

'No!' Sérgio screamed, with tears flowing down his cheeks. It just wasn't Portugal's day and their remaining nine players knew it now.

At the final whistle, Luís pounded the grass with his fists. He couldn't believe it. It was a horrible way to end his first World Cup.

'You'll be back!' the Portugal coaches said, trying to comfort him.

At that moment, however, Luís was beyond comfort. It was only once the disappointment had faded that he could look ahead to a next World Cup. If he stayed fit and healthy, he could make it to the 2006 tournament. He would get one last chance.

CHAPTER 20

RUNNING RIOT WITH RONALDO II

'So, who do you think will be our next Galáctico?' Luís asked in pre-season training.

'David Beckham?' Raúl suggested.

'Thierry Henry?' Zinedine guessed.

'No, I think it'll be Ronaldo,' Roberto Carlos said confidently.

Zinedine laughed and rolled his eyes. 'You're only saying that because you're both Brazilian!'

But Roberto Carlos was right – in September 2002, Ronaldo became Real Madrid's new star striker. The fans were really excited about the news and so was Luís. At Barcelona, they had formed a perfect partnership and now they were going to play together again.

'I've missed your crosses!' Ronaldo admitted as they hugged.

'And I've missed your goals!' Luís replied happily.

Ronaldo made his debut as a substitute against Alavés. The atmosphere was nice and relaxed as they entered the dressing room before the match. The shirts were hanging in a row along the wall – '3 R. CARLOS', '5 ZIDANE', '7 RAÚL', '10 FIGO' and now '11 RONALDO'. With so many superstars in the same team, Real Madrid had every reason to feel very confident.

'Don't worry,' Zinedine told their new teammate, 'we'll make sure we're winning comfortably by the time you come on!'

Roberto Carlos passed to Zinedine, who curled the ball into the top corner. 1–0!

Luís stepped up to take a penalty and sent the keeper the wrong way. 2–0!

On the bench, Ronaldo clapped and smiled. 'I think I'm going to enjoy playing with these guys!' he said to himself.

Eventually, the big moment arrived. As Ronaldo ran onto the field, the Real Madrid fans stood up and cheered his name. They couldn't wait to see what he would do.

They only had to wait one minute. When Roberto Carlos crossed the ball from the left, Ronaldo chested the ball down and fired it past the keeper. 3–1!

'Welcome to the team!' Zinedine shouted as all the players jumped on their new star.

It was party time at the Bernabéu. Luís beat the offside trap and chipped the ball cheekily over the keeper with the outside of his right foot. 4–1!

Goooooooooooooooooooooaaaaaaaaaaaaaaalllllllllll llllllllllllllllll!!!!!!!!!!!!!!!

Ronaldo raced over to congratulate Luís. 'I see – is this a competition now?' he asked with a grin.

Friendly competition was good. Real Madrid's top talents were working together to get the best out of each other. With ten minutes to go, Ronaldo scored again to make it 5–1.

Could anyone stop the Galácticos? Not in La Liga,

they couldn't. Real Madrid were 1–0 down against Real Betis when their superstars saved the day. Raúl scored first, then Luís, then Zinedine and finally Ronaldo.

'We're like The Beatles!' Luís joked as the fearsome foursome celebrated yet another victory.

'Hey, what about me?' Roberto Carlos asked grumpily. 'Just because I'm a defender, that doesn't mean I'm not a Galáctico!'

'Yeah, and what about me?' Claude Makélélé added.

'And me!' cried out Iker Casillas.

Real Madrid's biggest challenge was the Champions League. Could they win it for a second year in a row? No team had done that since AC Milan in the late 1980s, but Luís believed in his special teammates.

'Come on, if anyone can do it, the Galácticos can!' he cheered.

In the quarter-finals, they took on the mighty Manchester United. They had lots of superstars too, including David Beckham, Ryan Giggs and Paul

Scholes. Real would have to play their best attacking football to win.

Luís got the ball on the left wing and showed off his fancy footwork against Gary Neville. There was no way through, however, so he passed inside to Zinedine. They had to be patient. Zinedine thought about shooting but instead, he passed back to Luís, who was now in space on the edge of the box.

Luís could see that Fabien Barthez, Manchester United's goalkeeper, was off his line. He had to think fast, so fast that he couldn't even take a touch to control it. He coolly curled the ball up over Barthez and into the top right corner.

Goooooooooooooooooooooaaaaaaaaaaaaalllllllllllllllll llllllllll!!!!!!!!!!!!!!!!!!!

Luís punched the air as he ran over to the fans. He was the Real Madrid hero once more. What a delightful feeling it was to score a big goal in such a big game.

'Be honest – was that a cross or a shot?' Roberto Carlos teased him.

Luís sighed dramatically, 'How can you even ask

me that question? How long have you known me? If I wanted to cross it, the ball would have landed right on Raúl's head!'

Zinedine passed to Raúl, who spun and shot. 2–0!

Luís dribbled down the right wing and pulled the ball back to Raúl. 3–0!

Real Madrid were on fire, and Ronaldo hadn't even scored. Yet. In the second leg at Old Trafford, the Brazilian helped himself to a hat-trick. After crushing Manchester United, the Galácticos were on their way to the semi-finals.

Their opponents were Juventus, Zinedine's old club. 'Please guys, we have to win this,' he told his teammates. 'Otherwise, Buffon and Del Piero will mock me forever!'

Luís passed to Ronaldo, who flicked it over to Raúl. Raúl played the one-two and Ronaldo shot into the bottom corner. 1–0!

'What a finish!' Luís screamed, giving his friend a big hug.

Zinedine looked relieved but the job wasn't done. Seconds before half-time, Juventus scored an important away goal. Even when Roberto Carlos made it 2–1, the Real Madrid players still weren't satisfied.

'We need to get a goal in Italy,' Luís argued. 'We can't just sit back and defend. That's not our style. Let's do what we do best – attack!'

Unfortunately, they only scored in the last minute of the match, when Juventus were already 3–0 up. It was a total catastrophe for Real Madrid. Their defenders had failed and so had their attackers, even Mr Reliable. To make matters worse, Luís had even missed a penalty. He never normally missed a penalty.

'Hey, we'll come back even stronger next year,' Roberto Carlos said, trying to comfort his devastated teammate.

Luís nodded glumly. A fourth Spanish League title helped to ease his pain a little, but he always wanted more. Perhaps Euro 2004 would be the answer.

CHAPTER 21

EURO 2004

4 July 2004

Thirteen years after their Golden Generation won the FIFA Youth World Championship, Portugal were back at Lisbon's Estádio da Luz to play in another final. This time, it was the final of Euro 2004 and Luís was the captain of his country. He was just one step away from lifting an international trophy.

'Come on!' he clapped and cheered as he led his team out onto the pitch.

Of that original Golden Generation, only Luís and Rui remained. They now lined up alongside the stars of José Mourinho's Champions League-winning Porto team – Ricardo Carvalho, Maniche and Deco – and one massive star of the future. Cristiano Ronaldo was still only nineteen years old, but he was already taking Europe by storm with his skill and speed. And who had been his childhood hero? Luís, of course.

'I can't believe that I'm playing in the same team as you,' Cristiano said, completely star-struck. 'Watching you at Sporting inspired me to become a winger!'

'Wow, thanks for making me feel so old!' Luís joked back.

With a mix of experience and youth, and the home crowd behind them, Portugal wouldn't get a better chance to win a major tournament. The only obstacle standing in their way were Greece, the team that had beaten them in their first group match, and the team they now faced again in the final.

Since that bad start, however, Portugal had found their form. They had beaten Russia, Spain, England and the Netherlands on the way to the final. Cristiano and Maniche got most of the goalscoring glory, but Luís was the leader, the one who made the magic happen. The team relied on their captain's composure and creativity.

Just before the match kicked off, Luís closed his eyes and listened to the noise of the 62,000 fans.

The volume was already ear-splitting, and the football hadn't even begun. What would it be like if Portugal lifted the trophy?

'*When* we lift the trophy,' he corrected himself. It was going to be absolutely amazing. All of Portugal's most famous people were there watching in the stadium, including the president and 'The King', Eusébio. It would be the country's proudest football moment.

Unfortunately, not all of the players were as calm under pressure as Luís. The team got off to a shaky start, with panic at both ends of the pitch. The defenders were worried about making mistakes and the attackers were desperate to be the heroes. As Maniche crossed into the box, Miguel and Pauleta both went for the same ball and knocked into each other!

'Slow down!' Luís shouted, pushing his hands towards the grass. Portugal wouldn't become the Champions of Europe if they kept playing like that. 'Take your time and think!'

At half-time, the score was still 0–0. The pressure was building around the stadium. The fans wanted something to celebrate. The Portugal players were feeling frustrated but their manager Luiz Felipe Scolari told them not to worry.

'Greece want you to feel frustrated! Their plan is to defend deep and then catch you on the counter-attack. They're waiting for you to lose your focus out there – so don't!'

With Luís on the ball, Portugal looked more dangerous, but the attack still wasn't clicking together. When he curled a great cross towards the back post, no-one made the run.

'Someone!' Luís cried out in exasperation.

At the other end, Greece won a corner and Angelos Charisteas scored. 1–0! Three-quarters of the stadium fell silent. Portugal's defenders started arguing with each other, but Luís stepped in.

'It doesn't matter now,' he told them. 'What matters is scoring an equaliser!'

Luís moved into the middle of midfield to run the game for Portugal. His pass set up Cristiano, but his shot was saved. A few minutes later, Luís dribbled into the penalty area. The fans were up on their feet, cheering on their hero, but he struck the ball straight at the goalkeeper.

What a chance! Luís shook his head. He could do so much better than that.

As the minutes ticked by, Portugal became more and more desperate to score. Rui came off the bench but even that didn't help. They blazed the ball high over the bar time and time again. Luís tried his best to keep the players calm, but that wasn't easy when the big scoreboard above them showed 'PORTUGAL 0 GREECE 1'.

As if Luís's night couldn't get any worse, a man ran onto the pitch and threw a Barcelona flag at him. He didn't react at all. Perhaps it could spur him on to save the day for his country.

Nuno passed to Luís in the penalty area. He had his back to goal and three defenders around him, but with a beautiful bit of skill, Luís turned and hit a left-foot shot. As the ball flew past the keeper's outstretched arm, the whole of Portugal got ready to celebrate. Surely, this was the goal they needed… but it curled just wide of the far post.

'Nooo!' Luís screamed. That was it – his last big chance to score.

At the final whistle, the Greece players sank to their knees in delight. Some of the Portugal players fell to the floor in anguish, but others, like Luís, just stood and stared at the ground. He couldn't believe what had happened. In that horrible moment, losing in the final felt worse than going out in the first round. It was so painful to get so close.

Luís walked over to Cristiano, who had floods of tears running down his cheeks.

'This is just the start for you,' he said, putting an arm around his young teammate's shoulder. 'Remember this feeling and lead Portugal to glory next time!'

For Luís, however, it was the end. He had tried so hard to bring joy to his nation but ultimately, he had failed. Now, it was the next generation's turn to try. Luís was still only thirty-one but he felt like he had nothing left to give.

'It's time for me to take a break,' he told the Portuguese people a month later. 'I don't know if it will be forever.'

CHAPTER 22

ONE LAST TRY

Thankfully for Portugal, it wasn't forever. Less than a year later, Luís was back in the national squad.

'I couldn't just sit at home and watch you struggle against Slovakia, could I?' he joked happily with his teammates.

It was good to be back. Luís hadn't enjoyed his international retirement at all. He missed the thrill of representing his country. After so many years of trying, was he really ready to give up on his dream? He wasn't the kind of player who said no to a challenge.

The more he thought about it, the more Luís realised that he still had unfinished business. At the

2006 World Cup in Germany, he would still only be thirty-three. There was still life in his old legs, and hopefully he could help guide Portugal's next generation to glory. Surely, it was worth one last try.

When Luís returned, his old captain's armband was waiting for him. 'Welcome back, skipper!' Pauleta said, handing it over. Since his retirement, Pauleta had been sharing the role with Costinha.

Luís's comeback match was a very special one. Not only did Portugal win, but Luís also became the most-capped player in his country's history.

'See, it was totally worth returning!' Cristiano grinned.

It certainly looked that way. Portugal cruised through World Cup qualification without losing a single match. In attack, Cristiano was getting better and better, while Pauleta was on fire. In defence, Ricardo Carvalho and Fernando Meira were as solid as a brick wall.

As the squad travelled to Germany for the World Cup, Luís felt more determined than ever. 'This is it,' he told himself. 'It's now or never!'

In the first match against Angola, Luís burst forward from midfield. Yes, there was certainly still life in his old legs! He knocked the ball past the defender and then ran onto it. Inside the penalty area, Luís crossed to Pauleta for an easy finish. 1–0!

Even in his excitement, Pauleta didn't forget about the amazing assist. He ran towards Luís, pointing and smiling.

'Thanks, I'm so glad you're here!' he cheered.

'Me too!' Luís replied.

Portugal were off to a winning start and it was all thanks to their captain. What would Luís do next?

Against Iran, he dribbled forward once more. He was playing with so much confidence. This time, Luís cut in from the left wing, pretended to shoot and passed across to Deco. Deco sent a super-strike into the top corner. 1–0!

Later on, Luís attacked down the left again. He was making life so difficult for his opponents. As he entered the penalty area, the defender lunged in with a clumsy tackle. Penalty! Cristiano took it and scored. 2–0!

Cristiano fell to his knees and roared up at Luís, who roared right back at him. Portugal's stars were united and focused on winning the World Cup.

Cristiano didn't play in the last group game against Mexico, but Captain Luís played eighty minutes. Only once victory was secured did he take a well-deserved rest.

'This is my last tournament,' Luís explained to his manager Scolari, 'so I want to play as much as possible, please!'

Luís got his wish. He played almost every minute of Portugal's tough battle against the Netherlands. In the quarter-final against England, he was only taken off just before extra time.

'Go out there and get the winning goal!' Luís urged his replacement, Hélder Postiga.

Unfortunately, he couldn't, and the match went to penalties. It was Euro 2004 all over again. Portugal had won that time – could they do it again? Luís was gutted to miss out on another shoot-out.

'I should be out there taking one,' he moaned to Pauleta. 'That's what captains do!'

Instead, all Luís could do was encourage and inspire his teammates. 'Come on, you can do it!' he yelled. 'One last push!'

When Cristiano scored the winning spot-kick, Luís ran onto the pitch, still wearing a blue bib over his Portugal shirt.

'Yes, Cris!' he cheered. 'We're into the semi-finals!'

Portugal were having their best World Cup since the glory days of Eusébio. In 1966, they had lost to England in the semi-finals. Forty years later, they had just beaten England in the quarter-finals. Could they now go all the way and win it?

Luís believed. Finally, he felt like he was living his international dream. Cristiano was in tears again, but this time, they were tears of joy.

In the semi-final, Portugal faced France. It was a rematch of the Euro 2000 semi-final – Luís vs his Real Madrid teammate Zinedine Zidane. That time, Zinedine had come out on top. Luís would do everything possible to stop that from happening again.

'Let's show the world that we've learnt our lessons from Euro 2000 and 2004,' he told his teammates in the dressing room. 'I want cool, calm heads all over the pitch and I want revenge! Yes?'

'Yes!' his teammates boomed back.

Portugal didn't panic, even when Zinedine scored another penalty. Luís couldn't believe that history was repeating itself.

'Hey, heads up! We've still got plenty of time,' he reassured his teammates.

Luís was a man on a mission but France defended well, and Portugal couldn't score. Pauleta shot wide and Luís headed over the bar. Despite their best efforts, their World Cup dream was over.

'At least we got to the semi-finals,' Pauleta argued. 'Only one other Portugal team can say that!'

That was true – they had plenty to be proud of. Luís was glad that he had given it one last try. He had no regrets.

It was now time to let the nation's next generation take over but first, there was a third-place play-off against Germany. Luís started on the bench and by the time he came on, Portugal were 3–0 down. There was nothing left to play for, except pride.

'Here,' Pauleta said, returning the captain's armband to Luís.

The whole crowd cheered – the Portugal fans *and* the Germany fans. It was an emotional moment for everyone. One of football's greatest players was hanging up his international boots.

Luís wasn't quite finished yet, however. He raced down the right wing one last time and delivered one of his trademark curling crosses. Nuno was there at the back post with a diving header. 3–1!

After 127 caps for his country, it was the perfect way for Luís to say goodbye.

CHAPTER 23

INTER MILAN

Luís was the first Galáctico to arrive at Real Madrid, and he was also the first to leave. In 2005, after five amazing seasons at the Bernabéu, he decided that it was time to move on. At the age of thirty-two, he wanted one last challenge in his incredible football career.

But where would he go? Luís liked the idea of England but in the end, he decided on Italy. Exactly ten years after he had nearly joined Juventus and Parma, Luís joined Inter Milan.

'This time, I only signed for one team, I promise!' he joked with the club chairman, Massimo Moratti.

Luís received a warm welcome in Italy. He was

Inter's big signing of the 2005 summer. With Luís
on the wing and the Brazilian Adriano up front, they
hoped to finally win the Italian League title for the
first time since 1989.

'Are you following us?' Esteban Cambiasso teased
Luís. Inter had bought three Argentinians from
Real Madrid – Esteban, Santiago Scolari and Walter
Samuel. It was nice to see so many familiar, friendly
faces on the training ground. Luís felt at home
straight away.

He wasn't there for a nice holiday, however. Luís
had joined Inter to win lots more trophies. Serie A
was no longer the superstar league it had been in the
1990s, but there were still plenty of top teams and
top players.

Inter's local rivals, AC Milan, had Paolo Maldini,
Kaká, Andriy Shevchenko and Luís's old friend Rui.

Juventus had Gianluigi Buffon, Zlatan Ibrahimović,
Alessandro Del Piero and Pavel Nedvěd. Luís knew
all about them. They had knocked his Real Madrid
team out of the Champions League.

Luís settled in brilliantly. Against Parma, he made a

run down the right and Juan Sebastián Verón passed to him. Luís dribbled into the penalty area and fired the ball into the bottom corner.

Goooooooooooooooooooaaaaaaaaaaaaallllllllllllllllll lllllllllll!!!!!!!!!!!!!!!!!!!!!

The stadium went wild and so did Luís. He ran towards the Inter fans, waving his right arm in the air. It was his first goal for his new club.

'Right, let's win the league!' he told Adriano.

It was the start of four special years in Italy. In his first year, Luís scored six goals and won the League and Cup double. As club captain Javier Zanetti lifted the trophies, blue confetti flew up into the sky above the San Siro. On the stage behind him, Luís and his teammates danced and sang.

Alè Alè Alè Inter Alè!

Winning was the greatest feeling in the world. It didn't matter how old Luís was, or how successful he'd become. A trophy was still a trophy. He still felt just as excited as he had felt during his early football days back in Almada. That buzz was why Luís kept playing the beautiful game.

'I never want to stop!' he admitted to Esteban.

'Don't even think about it,' his friend replied. 'We need you!'

Inter certainly needed Luís in the Italian Super Cup Final against Roma. After forty minutes, the Italian Champions were 3–0 down.

As the third goal went in, some of his teammates lay sprawled out on the grass. A stunned silence spread around the San Siro. Luís, however, wasn't giving up. Years of experience told him that the match wasn't over yet.

'Come on, we can still turn this around!' he called out.

With Luís pulling the strings in midfield, Inter Milan fought back. 3–1, then 3–2, then 3–3! The atmosphere in the stadium switched from despair to hope in the space of thirty minutes. Now, they just needed a winning goal.

In extra time, Inter Milan won a free kick just outside the penalty area. Luís grabbed the ball and no-one argued with him. After a short run-up, he swung the ball over the wall and into the corner of the net. The Roma goalkeeper threw himself across his goal, but he couldn't quite reach it.

Goooooooooooooaaaaaaaaaaaaaaaaaaaaaallllllllllllllllllllllllllll!!!!!!!!!!!!!!!!!!!!!

He had done it! Luís raced over to celebrate with Santiago and the other substitutes. Soon, he was at the centre of a huge team hug.

'What a hero!' new signing Zlatan Ibrahimović shouted as he piled on top.

Inter went on to win Serie A another three times in a row. Four Spanish League titles and now four Italian League titles – Luís needed to get a bigger box for all his winners' medals!

Although he was still a key part of the team, though, Luís was slowing down, season by season. He had been so lucky with injuries throughout his career but by the age of thirty-five, every knock hurt a little more. It took longer to recover after every match he played.

Inter Milan's new manager José Mourinho looked after Luís carefully.

'We need legends like you to stay around for as

long as possible,' Mourinho told him.

Luís loved playing for the club but he knew that his playing career was coming to an end. He wanted to go out on a high, rather than fade away or move to an easier league. When Inter won the 2008–09 Serie A title, Luís made his decision.

'I am leaving football, not Inter,' he told the Italian media. 'I will never forget my time here as a player, and after my retirement, I want to keep helping the club to become even greater.'

Luís's last match for Inter was at home against Atalanta on 31 May 2009. The atmosphere in the San Siro was an odd mix of joy and sadness. On the one hand, the club was celebrating another league title, but on the other, it was saying goodbye to one of its favourite players.

Javier walked out onto the pitch as captain but before kick-off, he handed the armband to Luís. 'I want you to wear this today – you deserve it!'

Luís was overwhelmed by his friend's kindness. 'Thank you, it would be an honour,' he managed to say eventually.

It was time for one last masterclass. Luís raced down the right wing, with two defenders trailing behind him. He looked up and crossed into the danger zone. The goalkeeper cleared it, but only as far as Sulley Muntari. 1–0!

'See, you've still got it!' Javier laughed as he high-fived Luís.

His grand finale ended just before half-time. As Luís left the field, everyone stood and clapped – the players on the pitch, the coaches on the bench, and the fans in the stands. It was a very emotional moment for Luís as he hugged each of his Inter teammates.

'We're going to miss you!' Mourinho told him.

'I'll miss you too!' he replied.

Luís waved and blew kisses to the crowd. It was a beautiful way to end a remarkable career.

PORTUGAL'S NEXT NUMBER 7

When Luís retired from international football, he knew that he was leaving Portugal in safe hands. His Golden Generation had achieved so much, but the World Cup trophy remained just beyond their reach. They had led the way and now it was time for the next generation to follow.

Portugal's future looked brighter than ever. There were lots of new stars coming through like Nani, Ricardo Quaresma, João Moutinho, and, of course, Cristiano. Cristiano would be Portugal's next leader and their next Number 7, and Luís was sure that he would do a brilliant job.

Ever since Cristiano's international debut in 2003,

Luís had looked after him, encouraging his skills and passing on all of his advice and experience. Now, he was passing on his shirt too.

'Are you sure?' Cristiano asked. It would be an amazing honour to follow in his hero's footsteps. 'You're the reason I picked the Number Seven shirt for Manchester United!'

Luís smiled. 'I'm glad you like it because it's your number for Portugal too now. Good luck – and go win us the World Cup!'

Turn the page for a sneak preview of
another brilliant football story by
Matt and Tom Oldfield. . .

CRISTIANO RONALDO

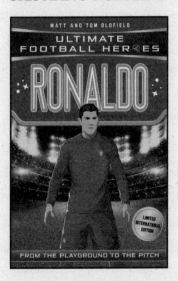

Available now!

CHAPTER 1

EUROPEAN GLORY

Cristiano had already won so many trophies during his amazing career – one Spanish league title, two Spanish cups, three Premier League titles, three English cups, three Champions League trophies and three Ballon d'Ors. But he still felt something was missing. That something was an international trophy with Portugal.

And on 10 July 2016, he was one step away from achieving that dream. With his confidence and goals, Cristiano had led his team all the way to the Euro 2016 final. At the Stade de France, Portugal faced a France team with home advantage and world-class players like Paul Pogba and Antoine Griezmann.

Portugal were the underdogs, but they had the best player in Europe – Cristiano. And he had never been more determined to win.

After their coach, Fernando Santos, had given his team talk in the dressing room, it was time for the senior players to speak. Nani went first and then it was Cristiano's turn.

'We've done so well to get this far,' their captain told them. 'One more win and we will go down in history. We will return home as heroes!'

The whole squad cheered. Together they could become the champions of Europe.

Cristiano stood with his eyes closed for the Portuguese national anthem. He didn't mumble the words; he shouted them at the top of his voice. He loved his country and he wanted to do them proud on the pitch.

After seven minutes, Cristiano got the ball just inside the French half. As he turned to attack, Dimitri Payet fouled him. The game carried on but Cristiano was still on the ground, holding his left knee and screaming in agony.

Oww!

As the physios used the magic spray and rubbed his knee with an ice pack, Cristiano winced. The injury didn't look good. He put his hands to his face to hide the tears.

Dimitri came over to say sorry for his tackle, but Cristiano was too upset to reply. Eventually, he stood up and limped off the field. On the touchline, he tested his leg – it didn't feel good but he wanted to keep playing.

'Are you sure?' João Mário said to him as he walked back onto the pitch.

'I have to try!' Cristiano told him.

But a minute later, he collapsed to the ground. On his big day, Cristiano was in too much pain to continue. He kept shaking his head – he couldn't believe his bad luck.

'You have to go off,' Nani told him, giving his friend a hug. 'We'll do our skipper proud, I promise!'

Cristiano wasn't ready to give up yet, though. The physios put a bandage around his knee and he went back on again. But when he tried to run, he had to stop. He signalled to the bench: 'I need to come off'.

He ripped off his captain's armband. 'Wear this,' Cristiano said to Nani, putting the armband on him. 'And win this final!'

'Yes, we'll win this for you!' Pepe shouted.

As he was carried off on a stretcher, Cristiano cried and cried. The most important match of his life was over.

It was 0–0 at half-time and Cristiano was there in the dressing room to support his teammates. 'Stick together and keep fighting hard!' he told them.

In the second-half, he was there on the bench, biting his fingernails and, in his head, kicking every ball. Every time Portugal nearly scored, he was up on his feet ready to celebrate. Just before striker Éder went on as a sub, Cristiano looked him in the eyes and said, 'Be strong. You're going to score the winner.'

But after ninety minutes, it was still 0–0. Cristiano walked around giving encouragement to the tired players. It was tough not being out on the pitch, but he could still play his part. After 109 minutes, Éder got the ball, shrugged off the French defender and sent a rocket of a shot into the bottom corner.

Goooooooooooooaaaaaaaaallllllllllllllllllll!!!!!!!!!!!

Cristiano went wild, throwing his arms in the air and jumping up and down. The whole Portugal squad celebrated together. They were so close to victory now.

For the last ten minutes, Cristiano stood with Santos as a second manager. He hobbled along the touchline, shouting instructions to the players.

Run! Defend! Take your time!

At the final whistle, Cristiano let out a howl of happiness as the tears rolled down his cheeks again. He hugged each of his teammates and thanked them.

'No, thank *you!*' Éder said to him. 'Without you, I wouldn't have scored that goal!'

'I told you we'd do it!' Pepe laughed.

Cristiano took his shirt off and threw it into the crowd. They had to give him another one so that he could do his captain's duty – collecting the Euro 2016 trophy.

He climbed the steps slowly, giving high-fives to

the fans he passed. The trophy had red and green ribbons, the colours of Portugal's flag. As Cristiano lifted the trophy, the whole team cheered. He kissed it and then passed it on to the other players. No words could describe the joy that Cristiano was feeling.

It was at Manchester United and Real Madrid that he became a superstar, but Cristiano's incredible journey to the top of world football had begun at home in Portugal, with his family, on the island of Madeira. And so the Euro 2016 triumph was a way of saying thanks, for when life wasn't always easy growing up.

Without a difficult start in life, perhaps Cristiano wouldn't have had his amazing hunger to be the best, which turned a special gift into years of glory.

LUÍS FIGO
HONOURS

Sporting Lisbon
🏆 Portuguese Cup: 1994–95

Barcelona
🏆 La Liga: 1997–98, 1998–99
🏆 Copa Del Rey: 1997, 1998
🏆 Spanish Super Cup: 1996
🏆 UEFA Cup Winners' Cup: 1997
🏆 UEFA Super Cup: 1997

Real Madrid
🏆 La Liga: 2000–01, 2002–03
🏆 Spanish Super Cup: 2001, 2003

🏆 UEFA Champions League: 2002

🏆 UEFA Super Cup: 2002

🏆 Intercontinental Cup: 2002

Inter Milan

🏆 Serie A: 2005–06, 2006–07, 2007–08, 2008–09

🏆 Coppa Italia: 2006

🏆 Italian Super Cup: 2006, 2008

Portugal

🏆 UEFA European Under-17 Football Championship: 1989

🏆 FIFA U-20 World Cup: 1991

Individual

🏆 UEFA Under-21 Championship Golden Player: 1994

🏆 Portuguese Golden Ball: 1994

🏆 Portuguese Footballer of the Year: 1995, 1996, 1997, 1998, 1999, 2000

🏆 La Liga Foreign Player of the Year: 1999, 2000, 2001

- 🏆 UEFA European Championship Team of the Tournament: 2000, 2004
- 🏆 Ballon d'Or: 2000
- 🏆 FIFA World Player of the Year: 2001
- 🏆 UEFA Team of the Year: 2003
- 🏆 UEFA Champions League top assist provider: 2004–05
- 🏆 FIFA World Cup All-Star Team: 2006

FIGO

78 & 10

THE FACTS

NAME: Luís Filipe Madeira Caeiro Figo

DATE OF BIRTH: 4 November 1972

AGE: 45

PLACE OF BIRTH: Almada

NATIONALITY: Portuguese

BEST FRIEND: Rui Costa

CURRENT CLUB: Barcelona, Real Madrid and Inter Milan

POSITION: RW

THE STATS

Height (cm):	180
Club appearances:	795
Club goals:	133
Club trophies:	22
International appearances:	127
International goals:	32
International trophies:	0
Ballon d'Ors:	1

★ ★ ★ **HERO RATING: 91** ★ ★ ★

GREATEST MOMENTS

Type and search the web links to see the magic for yourself!

11 NOVEMBER 1992, PORTUGAL 2-1 BULGARIA

https://www.youtube.com/watch?v=kdzsz2fYuO0&t=2265s

Playing for Portugal was a dream come true for Luís. A year after making his senior debut, he scored his first international goal in a friendly match against Bulgaria. This time, Luís didn't curl the ball into the corner of the net with his wicked right foot. Instead, he flicked it in with a brilliant header! Luís had only just turned twenty and he was already well on his way to the top.

28 JUNE 1997,
BARCELONA 3-2 REAL BETIS

https://www.youtube.com/watch?v=I1YsiyR4wC0&t=108s

It didn't take long for Luís to become a fans' favourite
at Barcelona. In the 1997 Copa del Rey Final, he stole
the show with two goals. His matchwinner was a lucky
tap-in, but the first was a long-range wondergoal after a
mazy dribble. Luís showed that Ronaldo wasn't the only
superstar at the club.

12 JUNE 2000,
PORTUGAL 3-2 ENGLAND

https://www.youtube.com/watch?v=tMn7I3rImWk

At Euro 2000, Portugal's Golden Generation got off
to a terrible start. England took an early 2–0 lead,
but luckily Luís was there to lead the fightback. As
he dribbled towards the goal, the defenders backed
away in fear. From thirty yards out, Luís unleashed
a ferocious strike that flew into the top corner. After
that, Portugal won the match 3–2.

8 APRIL 2003,
REAL MADRID 3-1 MANCHESTER UNITED

https://www.youtube.com/watch?v=nuk2bz1FHi0
Luís had so many golden moments with the Galácticos
– Raúl, Roberto Carlos, Zinedine Zidane and Ronaldo.
This goal in the Champions League quarter-final against
Manchester United was perhaps Luís's best in a Real
Madrid shirt. After exchanging passes with Zidane on
the edge of the box, he coolly chipped the ball over the
goalkeeper and into the far corner of the net.

26 AUGUST 2006,
INTER MILAN 4-3 ROMA

https://www.youtube.com/watch?v=8aG0hD1Ab4k
When Luís moved from Real Madrid to Inter Milan,
he didn't slow down at all. In the Italian Super Cup,
they found themselves 3–0 down after 34 minutes.
But Luís and his teammates didn't give up at all.
forty minutes later, it was 3–3 and in extra-time, Luís
scored an amazing free-kick to win the game and yet
another trophy.

PLAY LIKE YOUR HEROES

ULTIMATE WING WIZARD:
THE LUÍS FIGO DRIBBLE AND CROSS

SEE IT HERE You Tube

https://www.youtube.com/watch?v=nvnvBJzhtoo

STEP 1: Get the ball on the wing and dribble forward at full speed. Attack and be brave!

Step 2: If there's a defender in front of you, dazzle them with your full range of stepovers. Keep them guessing – right foot or left foot? Will you cut inside or carry on down the line?

Step 3: Once you're ready to cross, look up and find your target. If in doubt, aim for the danger zone – the six-yard line, just out of the goalkeeper's reach.

Step 4: Put plenty of curl on your cross and just the right amount of power and height. You want to serve the ball up on a plate!

Step 5: Goal! Wait for the goalscorer to come and celebrate with you. You're the hero.

TEST YOUR KNOWLEDGE

QUESTIONS

1. Which international tournament changed Luís's life when he was nine years old?

2. Who were Luís's first two Portuguese football heroes?

3. What was the superstar sign that really impressed Aurélio Pereira during Luís's Sporting Lisbon trial?

4. Which Sporting defender tested Luís in training and gave him good advice?

5. Which future Real Madrid teammate did Luís play against in the final of the 1991 FIFA U-20 World Cup?

6. Which striker did Luís play with at both Barcelona and Real Madrid?

7. Who managed Luís in the Portugal Under-20s and senior team, as well as at Sporting Lisbon?

8. Luís wore the Number 7 shirt at Real Madrid – true or false?

9. How many Euros did Luís play in for Portugal?

10. How many World Cups did Luís play in for Portugal?

11. Who did Luís pass the Portugal Number 7 shirt on to?

Answers below. . . No cheating!

1. *The 1982 World Cup* 2. *Fernando Chalana and Paulo Futre* 3. *The calm, careful way that he tied his boot laces.* 4. *Pedro Venâncio* 5. *Roberto Carlos* 6. *Ronaldo* 7. *Carlos Queiroz* 8. *False – he wore Number 10 because Raúl already had the Number 7 shirt.* 9. *Three – 1996, 2000 and 2004* 10. *2 – 2002 and 2006* 11. *Cristiano Ronaldo*

This summer, your favourite football heroes will pull on their country's colours to go head-to-head for the ultimate prize – the World Cup.

Celebrate by making sure you have six of the best Ultimate Football Heroes, now with limited edition international covers!

COMING 31ST MAY

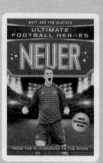

FOLLOW IN THE FOOTSTEPS OF LEGENDS. . .

Bridge the gap between past and present by stepping into the shoes of six classic World Cup heroes and reading their exciting stories – from the playground to the pitch, and to superstardom!

✦ COMING 31ST MAY ✦

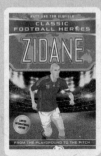